THE SCRIPTURAL JOURNEY

MALVIKA DHAWAN

Made with ♥ on the Notion Press Platform
www.notionpress.com

योगस्थः कुरु कर्माणि सङ्गं त्यक्त्वा धनञ्जय।

सद्धि्यसद्धि्योः समो भूत्वा समत्वं योग उच्यते।

yogasthaḥ kuru karmāṇi saṅgaṃ tyaktvā dhanañjaya

siddhyasiddhyoḥ samo bhūtvā samatvaṃ yoga ucyate

Meaning

Be steadfast in yoga, O Arjuna. Perform your duty and abandon all attachments to success or failure. Such evenness of mind is called yoga.

Contents

Author's Note

I am Malvika Dhawan—a passionate devotee of Indian mythology—and The Scriptural Journey marks my second book. Currently studying in Grade XI at Sri Chaitanya Techno School, Karnal, I have delved into over 60 books on Indian (Hindu) mythology, a subject that has fascinated me since early childhood.

My love for mythology began at the age of two, sparked by the animated film Krishna aur Kans. That small moment lit a lifelong flame. Over the years, I immersed myself in mythological TV serials such as Mahabharat, Suryaputra Karn, and Devon Ke Dev... Mahadev, eventually turning to books that deepened my understanding of our timeless scriptures and ancient heritage.

In March 2024, I had the immense pleasure of co-authoring my first book, ADIYOGI's Pearls of Wisdom, alongside my dear friend and creative partner, Arjun Rana. Our shared vision, unwavering dedication, and mutual fascination with Lord Shiva's teachings allowed us to channel our efforts into something truly meaningful. ADIYOGI's Pearls of Wisdom was our first step toward illuminating the eternal truths hidden within the words of the Destroyer—Lord Shiva. Together, we aspired to awaken readers to the deeper spiritual realities that often go unnoticed in our fast-paced world.

Working with Arjun was an experience filled with enthusiasm, learning, and countless discussions about the essence of life. Our collaboration was more than a writing process—it was a spiritual exploration, a bond that reflected our mutual respect for the sacred knowledge we were trying to present. We encouraged each other to think deeply, question everything, and ultimately shape a book that could serve as a guiding light for others.

With that foundation laid, I was inspired to write The Scriptural Journey—a natural progression from our earlier work, but this time a solo effort aimed at engaging younger minds. This quiz book contains 108 multiple-choice questions, divided into 12 chapters, each featuring 9 questions followed by an answer key with concise explanations. Each chapter also opens with a brief introduction to set the tone.

The goal of this book isn't merely to quiz; it's to inspire. It's a gentle effort to rekindle interest in Hindu mythology, especially among the youth. In an era where cultural values are increasingly overshadowed by material distractions, I believe this book can serve as both a learning tool and a spark for self-discovery.

I deeply value the support, feedback, and forgiveness of my readers should any errors remain in these pages. This journey—both mine and Arjun's—is far from over, and every bit of encouragement brings us closer to the next chapter.

With heartfelt gratitude,
Malvika Dhawan

DEBUT WORK

ADIYOGI's Pearls of Wisdom by Malvika &
Arjun

<u>ADIYOGI's Pearls ofWisdom</u> is a book that will enlighten its readers on the significance of life. It is a way of teaching the lessons of wisdom to its readers. This book will teach their readers the eternal truth, the goal of their life and the impact of Material Life on us.

This book is just a small step for us. Through this, we wish the knowledge and the wit of our readers will be enhanced. As you read further, you will understand the meaning of life and death, Cycle of Karma, importance of Education, Vedas, etc. and by the end the readers will be eligible to understand the difference between Material Life and the actual reality.

We hope you find this book motivating.

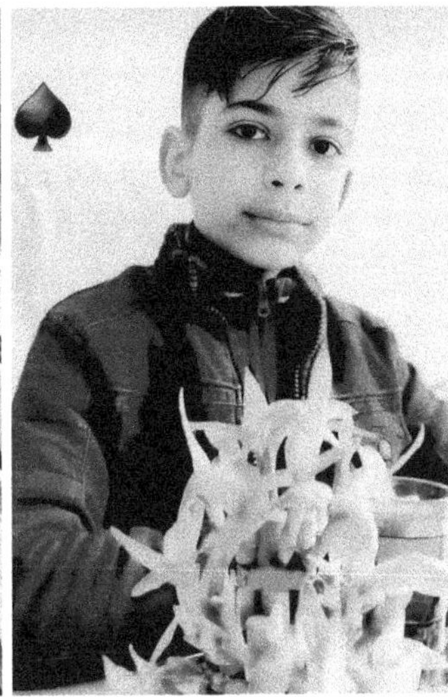

From the Author's Desk (Malvika & Arjun - Co-authors of ADIYOGI's Pearls of Wisdom)

From the moment we first discussed the idea of this book, we both felt an inner calling—an urge to explore, understand, and share the timeless teachings of Lord Shiva, the Adiyogi. Adiyogi's Pearls of Wisdom is more than a collection of words—it is the reflection of our shared passion, our spiritual curiosity, and our deep-rooted reverence for Hindu mythology.

We, Malvika and Arjun, come from same class and school, what unites us is a profound admiration for the divine figure of Lord Shiva—the cosmic force of transformation, the silent observer, the eternal yogi. Through countless conversations, research sessions, and hours of reflection, we embarked on this journey not as scholars, but as seekers.

Our goal in writing this book was simple yet profound: to offer readers a glimpse into the wisdom of Adiyogi that can illuminate everyday life. Shiva's words are not confined to ancient times—they are alive in our thoughts, actions, choices, and silences. His philosophy is not bound by religion; it is a universal message of detachment, awareness, inner strength, and the pursuit of truth.

As young voices in the literary world, we believe that spirituality must not be kept locked within the walls of temples or texts—it must be lived, questioned, and experienced. Through this book, we've attempted to present age-old teachings in a manner that resonates with today's reader, especially the youth, who often feel disconnected from our cultural roots.

This book is not a scholarly treatise, nor do we claim to be masters of the divine. We are merely messengers—transmitting a few pearls of Shiva's wisdom, in the hope that even one idea, one thought, or one insight may plant a seed in the reader's mind. If our words ignite a spark of curiosity, reflection, or transformation in even a single soul, we will consider our efforts worthwhile.

We are deeply grateful for the opportunity to walk this path together, to learn from each other, and to bring this book into the world. It is a small offering to the infinite—a humble bow to the Adiyogi.

With reverence and love,
Malvika & Arjun

PREFACE

<u>The Scriptural Journey</u> was conceived as a response to a growing need I observed in today's fast-paced, digitally driven world—an urgent need to reconnect with our roots.

While Indian mythology is vast and spiritually rich, it often remains underexplored by the younger generation. Despite being part of one of the world's oldest civilizations, many students today feel distant from the stories, symbols, and lessons embedded within our ancient scriptures. This book is a small step toward changing that.

Designed as an interactive learning experience, The Scriptural Journey features 108 multiple-choice questions carefully distributed across 12 chapters, each prefaced by a short introduction. The structure is meant to encourage both structured learning and spontaneous curiosity. Following the quiz sections, readers will find a comprehensive answer key with brief explanations to enrich understanding.

The idea behind this format is simple: to make the exploration of Hindu mythology engaging, accessible, and thought-provoking—especially for students and young readers who may be encountering these narratives for the first time. By framing learning through questions, the book aims to spark curiosity rather than provide rigid instruction. The questions range from basic to moderately advanced, encouraging both beginners and enthusiasts to reflect more deeply.

Though the tone is light and approachable, the underlying purpose is meaningful: to cultivate awareness of our cultural heritage, to inspire critical thought, and to plant the seeds of lifelong interest in India's spiritual and mythological traditions.

While this is not an academic textbook, care has been taken to ensure accuracy and clarity. Any errors that remain are entirely unintentional, and I remain open to feedback that helps improve future editions.

The Scriptural Journey invites you not just to answer questions—but to ask your own. To pause, reflect, and perhaps discover something timeless in the process.

Prologue

In every age, there are stories that survive the test of time—not because they are ancient, but because they are eternal. These stories speak not just of gods and battles, but of values, dilemmas, choices, and truths that continue to echo in the hearts of those who listen.

Indian mythology is not merely a collection of old tales. It is a mirror—reflecting the struggles and strengths of the human spirit. It is a compass—offering direction when the path ahead seems uncertain. It is a bridge—connecting generations through shared wisdom, rituals, and deeper meaning.

Yet today, as the world moves faster and distractions grow louder, many of us are drifting away from this vast ocean of knowledge. The myths that once shaped civilizations now sit quietly in dusty corners, waiting to be rediscovered.

The Scriptural Journey is a humble invitation to begin that rediscovery.

This book is not a test. It is not a competition. It is a journey—a guided exploration into the heart of Indian mythology through questions that provoke thought and awaken curiosity. Whether you know a little or a lot, every reader is welcome here. Each question is a doorway, and every answer is a spark—lighting the way toward deeper understanding.

The number 108 is sacred in Indian tradition, symbolizing completeness and spiritual unity. That is why this book offers 108 questions—divided into 12 chapters, each one a step on your path. Before each chapter, you'll find a short note to set the tone. And after the questions, you'll discover explanations that help bring the stories to life.

This journey is not about reaching a destination—it's about awakening something within you.

So turn the page not as a student, but as a seeker. Allow mythology to guide you, question you, and most importantly—transform you.

Let the journey begin.

I

Ganesha & his Siblings

Lord Ganesha, also known as Ganesh, is one of the most beloved and widely worshipped deities in Hinduism. Instantly recognizable by his elephant head and gentle demeanor, Ganesha is revered as the son of Lord Shiva and Goddess Parvati.

In the Hindu tradition, Ganesha holds a place of high spiritual significance as the God of Wisdom, Success, and Prosperity. He is often invoked at the beginning of rituals, ceremonies, and important life events to ensure the removal of obstacles and the smooth progression of endeavors. For this reason, he is also known by the name Vighnaharta, a Sanskrit term meaning "Lord of Obstacles" or more precisely, "Remover of Obstacles."

Ganesha's presence is not limited to religious practices alone—his symbolism permeates art, literature, and culture, often representing intellect, learning, and auspicious beginnings. Whether in temples, homes, or festivals, Ganesha is honored with deep devotion and affection.

According to certain mythological sources, Lord Ganesha is part of a divine family with several siblings. His elder brother is Kartikeya (also known as Murugan or Skanda), the god of war and victory. His elder sister, Ashok Sundari, is associated with beauty and grace. In some traditions and regional texts, deities such as Jalandhar, Andhaka, and Mansa Devi are also considered spiritual or divine siblings within the extended cosmic family.

Through centuries, Lord Ganesha has remained a symbol of strength through humility, wisdom through simplicity, and divine support in times of challenge. To worship Ganesha is to invite clarity, courage, and grace into one's life journey.

QUIZ

1. Which of the following jyotirlinga is associated with Skanda?
    (A) Mallikaarjuna
    (B) Trimbakeshwar
    (C) Baidyanath
    (D) Bhimashankar

2. Who among the following is the elder sister of Lord Ganesha?
    (A) Mansa
    (B) Ashok Sundari
    (C) Usha
    (D) Yogmaya

3. Name the epic written by Lord Ganesha from his broken tooth?
    (A) Shiv Puran
    (B) Mahabharata
    (C) Ramayana
    (D) None of These

4. How Godddess Parvati was blessed with Ashok Sundari?
    (A) Shivaling
    (B) Kalpavriskha
    (C) Kamdhenu
    (D) Parijata Tree

5. Who among the following was the teacher of Jalandhar?
    (A) Brihaspati
    (B) Kashyapa
    (C) Parshurama
    (D) Shurkacharya

6. Who among the following was born when goddess Parvati closed Shiva's eyes?
    (A) Andhaka
    (B) Vishahari
    (C) Lohitang
    (D) Jalandhar

7. Who was born from the sweat drop that fell on the ground when Lord Shiva performed Tandava?
    (A) Viraja
    (B) Jalandhar
    (C) Lohitang
    (D) None of These

8. Whom was Ashok Sundari married to? He belonged to which dynasty?
    (A) Ikshvaku; Suryavansh
    (B) Balram; Yaduvansh
    (C) Nahusha; Kuruvansh
    (D) Iravan; Nagavansh

9. Who among the following are the sons of Murgan?
(A) Ksema - Labha
(B) Sakha - Visakha
(C) Ashwini Kumars
(D) Nal - Neel

II

The Divine Forces of Creation & Knowledge

Lord Brahma, the revered God of Creation, holds a central position in Hindu cosmology. As the first among the Trimurti—the divine trinity consisting of Brahma (Creator), Vishnu (Preserver), and Shiva (Destroyer)—he is entrusted with the foundational act of creation, from which all life and order emerge.

Brahma is believed to have emerged from Lord Vishnu's navel. He is also known as Vagesa the Lord of Speech, and is credited with creating the universe and gifting humanity with the Vedas, the sacred scriptures that guide Hindu philosophy and ritual.

Despite his supreme creative role, Brahma is the least worshipped among the Trimurti in contemporary practice—a phenomenon rooted in various mythological tales and symbolic interpretations. Nonetheless, his role in shaping the cosmos remains pivotal and profound.

Alongside Brahma is his divine consort, Goddess Saraswati, the embodiment of wisdom, knowledge, and artistic expression. Saraswati is one of the Tridevi, the divine feminine counterparts to the Trimurti, along with Goddess Lakshmi and Goddess Parvati. Saraswati represents the refined and intellectual aspect of creation—language, literature, music, arts, and learning.

Her origins trace back to the Rigveda, where she is initially associated with a sacred river and later evolves into a celestial goddess of wisdom. Over the ages, she has remained one of the most venerated deities in Hindu tradition, especially among students, teachers, musicians, and scholars.

Saraswati is traditionally depicted with four arms, each holding an object of deep symbolic significance:

- A book, representing sacred knowledge and learning
- A rosary (mala), symbolizing meditation, focus, and spiritual discipline
- A water pot, denoting purity and the source of creative energy
- The veena, a classical musical instrument, signifying the harmony of arts and wisdom

Together, Lord Brahma and Goddess Saraswati form the divine pair responsible for both the creation of the world and the awakening of the mind. Where Brahma builds the structure of the universe, Saraswati breathes thought, meaning, and expression into it.

As you move forward through this chapter, reflect on how the powers of creation and knowledge go hand in hand—each incomplete without the other. The questions that follow will help you delve deeper into their stories, roles, and spiritual significance.

QUIZ

1. Who chopped of Lord Brahma's fifth head?
(A) Kali
(B) Vishnu
(C) Shiva
(D) Hiranyaksha

ॐ

2. Which of the following is a name of Goddess Saraswati?
    (A) Parshati
    (B) Padmakshi
    (C) Kamakhya
    (D) Manikarnika

ॐ

3. Which auspicious day is dedicated to Lord Brahma?
    (A) Guru Purnima
    (B) Makar Sankranti
    (C) Basant Panchami
    (D) Kartik Purnima

ॐ

4. Who among the following is the son of Lord Brahma and Goddess Saraswati?
    (A) Chitragupta
    (B) Chandra
    (C) Daksha
    (D) Both (A) and (C)

ॐ

5. Who among the following is the vahana of Goddess Saraswati?
    (A) Swan
    (B) Peacock
    (C) Horse
    (D) Crocodile

6. Where is the only Brahma temple located?
    (A) Varanasi
    (B) Gokul
    (C) Pushkar
    (D) Ujjain

7. Where is Gnana Saraswati temple located?
    (A) Kashmir
    (B) Basara
    (C) Ujjain
    (D) Varanasi

8. Whom does Lord Brahma worship to?
    (A) Vishnu
    (B) Shiva
    (C) Shakti
    (D) Lakshmi

9. Which festival is dedicated to goddess Saraswati?
(A) Baisakhi
(B) Lohri
(C) Makar Sankranti
(D) Basant Panchami

III

Guardians of Prosperity & Preservation

Among the most revered divine pairs in Hinduism, Goddess Lakshmi and Lord Vishnu (Narayana) embody the perfect balance of abundance and protection, prosperity and preservation. Together, they sustain the order and harmony of the cosmos.

Lakshmi, the radiant goddess of wealth, wisdom, fortune, and auspiciousness, is worshipped across India and beyond. She is especially honored during Diwali, the festival of lights, when devotees light lamps to invite her blessings into their homes. Representing both material and spiritual prosperity, Lakshmi symbolizes grace, generosity, and divine beauty.

She is typically depicted seated gracefully on a lotus flower, dressed in resplendent garments and adorned with gold ornaments. She has four arms, each symbolizing the four goals of human life (Purusharthas): dharma (righteousness), artha (wealth), kama (desires), and moksha (liberation). Often, she is shown surrounded by elephants, signifying royal power and fertility.

Lakshmi is believed to take on several avatars, each appearing alongside Vishnu's incarnations, reinforcing her role as his eternal consort. For instance, as Sita, she is the wife of Rama, and as Rukmini or Radha, she is the beloved of Krishna.

Lord Vishnu, also known as Narayana, is the Supreme Preserver in Hindu belief and the central deity of the Vaishnava tradition. As a principal member of the Trimurti—alongside Brahma the Creator and Shiva the Destroyer—Vishnu is entrusted with the protection and sustenance of the universe. His divine essence is described in sacred texts like the Ramayana and Mahabharata, where he is praised as Swayambhagavan, the self-manifested Supreme Being.

Vishnu is often depicted with a calm, compassionate expression, light blue skin, and four arms, each holding divine weapons and symbols:

- A Padma (lotus), symbolizing purity and spiritual enlightenment
- A Kaumodaki (mace), representing power and strength
- A Shankha (conch shell), the sound of cosmic truth
- A Sudarshana Chakra (discus), symbolizing the destruction of evil and protection of dharma

To restore balance on Earth, Vishnu has descended in various avatars, each with a divine mission. These ten incarnations, known as the Dashavatara, include Rama, Krishna, Narasimha, Parashurama, and the yet-to-come

Kalki, who is prophesied to appear in the future at the end of Kali Yuga to vanquish evil and restore righteousness.

Together, Sri Lakshmi–Narayana represent a cosmic partnership: Lakshmi nurtures and enriches life, while Vishnu protects and preserves it. Their union is not only divine but symbolic of the essential harmony between inner growth and outer order—between wealth and its rightful use, power and responsibility.

As you explore this chapter, reflect on how prosperity and preservation go hand in hand. The quiz questions that follow will guide you through the legends, symbols, and spiritual insights of this divine duo.

QUIZ

1. How many incarnations Lord Vishnu has?
(A) 10
(B) 24
(C) 14
(D) 18

2. Who among the following is the vahana of Goddess Lakshmi?
(A) Owl
(B) Horse
(C) Crocodile
(D) None of These

3. What is the name of Lord Vishnu's conch shell?
(A) Devdutt
(B) Panchajanya
(C) Manipushpaka
(D) Sharanga

4. Which day is dedicated to Goddess Lakshmi?
(A) Kartik Purnima
(B) Guru Purnima
(C) Lohri
(D) Sharad Purnima

5. Who provided Lord Vishnu with the Sudarshana Chakra?
    (A) Shiva
    (B) Lakshmi
    (C) Brahma
    (D) No one

ॐ

6. Who cursed Lord Vishnu of losing his wife Lakshmi that eventually became true during Ramayana?
    (A) Vedavati
    (B) Yogmaya
    (C) Rati
    (D) Vrinda

ॐ

7. Which of the following is a name of Goddess Lakshmi?
    (A) Bhargavi
    (B) Bhairavi
    (C) Narayani
    (D) Kushmanda

ॐ

8. Which incarnation was taken by Lord Vishnu after Goddess Lakshmi left Vaikuntha?
    (A) Hayagriva
    (B)Mohini
    (C) Srinivas
    (D) Nar-Narayana

ॐ

9. Which of the following is the name of the combined form of Lord Vishnu and Lord Shiva?
   (A) Harihara
   (B) Shankaranaryana
   (C) Manikantan
   (D) Both (A) and (B)

IV

Shiva–Shakti: The Cosmic Union

Which form was taken by Goddess Parvati to destroy a demon named Raktabeej? In the sacred symphony of Hindu mythology, few concepts are as profound and powerful as the divine union of Shiva and Shakti—eternal counterparts representing consciousness and cosmic energy, respectively. Together, they form the essence of creation, dissolution, transformation, and liberation.

Lord Shiva, also known as Mahadeva, is the Supreme Being in the Shaivism tradition and one of the principal deities of the Trimurti, alongside Brahma and Vishnu. He is revered as the Maha Rudra, the fierce master of time, destruction, and transcendence, yet also the most compassionate of yogis and gurus. Shiva embodies causeless auspiciousness, residing beyond the confines of time and matter.

Known as ADIYOGI—the first teacher—Shiva is the source of yogic wisdom and spiritual enlightenment. His third eye symbolizes higher perception and divine insight, while his blue throat, a result of swallowing the *Halahala* (poison) during the churning of the cosmic ocean, reflects his role as the savior of existence. Seated in deep meditation upon Mount Kailash, Shiva represents the still, infinite consciousness within all beings.

At his side is Goddess Parvati, his divine consort, also known as Mahadevi, Adi Shakti, and Abhaya Shakti—the primordial power that animates the universe. In the Shaktism tradition, she is venerated as the Supreme Goddess, the Para Brahman in feminine form. All goddesses—Lakshmi, Saraswati, Durga, Kali, Bhuvaneshwari, Tripura Sundari—are believed to be her manifestations.

Shakti is dynamic energy, the force that enlivens creation, sustains life, and brings transformation. Without Shakti, Shiva is inert; without Shiva, Shakti has no direction. Together, they are not separate entities, but two aspects of the same absolute reality.

Their divine union is not just a relationship of love, but a cosmic principle—a balance between stillness and movement, silence and expression, awareness and action. It is this sacred synergy of Shiv–Shakti that keeps the universe in motion and spiritual seekers on the path of liberation.

As you journey through this chapter, explore the deeper meanings behind their forms, legends, and significance. The questions that follow are designed to deepen your understanding of these cosmic forces and their relevance in our lives today.

QUIZ

1. There are how many jyotirlingas?
(A) 18
(B) 10
(C) 8
(D) 12

ॐ

2. Which form was taken by Goddess Parvati to destroy a demon named Raktabeej?
(A) Durga
(B) Kali
(C) Mahalsa
(D) Matsya

ॐ

3. Who cursed Lord Shiva that he would cut his sons' head, killing him?
(A) Kashyapa
(B) Bhrigu
(C) Atri
(D) Dadhichi

ॐ

4. Who cursed Goddess Parvati with infertility?
(A) Lakshmi
(B) Shachi
(C) Rati
(D) Ahilya

ॐ

5. Who was born when Lord Shiva opened his third eye in fury due to Indra?

    (A) Andhaka

    (B) Jalandhar

    (C) Lohitang

    (D) None of These

6. Which form did Goddess Parvati take to destroy Malla and Mani?

    (A) Matsya

    (B) Kumari

    (C) Katyayani

    (D) Mahalsa

7. Name the mother of the snake which is seen around Lord Shiva's neck?

    (A) Kadru

    (B) Diti

    (C) Vinata

    (D) Aditi

8. Which forms of Lord Shiva played a role in the epic – Mahabharata?

    (A) Sahadeva

    (B) Ashwathama

    (C) Hanuman

    (D) Both (B) and (C)

9. After Sati immolated herself, Lord Vishnu cut her body into how many peices, known as Shaktipeeth, from his Sudarshan Chakra?

(A) 108
(B) 24
(C) 52
(D) 1008

V

Rama's Journey: The Eternal Ideal

The Ramayana is one of the two great Itihasas (epic histories) of Hinduism, the other being the Mahabharata. Composed in Sanskrit and traditionally attributed to the sage Maharishi Valmiki, this timeless epic has shaped the cultural and spiritual fabric of India for thousands of years.

The Ramayana tells the inspiring story of Lord Rama, the righteous prince of Ayodhya, an ideal son, husband, and king—revered as the seventh avatar of Lord Vishnu. Through his life, the epic exemplifies the virtues of dharma (righteousness), sacrifice, truth, and devotion.

The story begins in the grand kingdom of Kosala, where Rama is born as the eldest son of King Dasharatha. When his stepmother Kaikeyi invokes a long-forgotten promise from the king, Rama is sent into exile for 14 years, renouncing the throne without hesitation. Accompanied by his devoted wife Sita and loyal brother Lakshmana, Rama ventures into the forests of ancient Bharatvarsha, encountering sages, demons, and divine beings along the way.

Tragedy strikes when the demon-king Ravana of Lanka abducts Sita, leading to a fierce and righteous war. Rama, with the help of Hanuman, Sugriva, and the Vanara Sena (monkey army), wages a battle of dharma against adharma. Ultimately, Ravana is defeated, Sita is rescued, and righteousness is restored.

Rama returns to Ayodhya, where his coronation (Pattabhisheka) is celebrated with divine glory, marking the beginning of Ram Rajya, the ideal kingdom symbolizing justice, harmony, and moral order.

More than a tale of heroism and love, the Ramayana is a spiritual guide. It teaches us that living a life of values—even in the face of trials—is the true path to greatness.

As you explore this chapter, dive into the profound characters and timeless lessons of the Ramayana. Let each question bring you closer to understanding the deeper essence of one of India's most beloved epics.

QUIZ

1. How many verse does Ramayana has?
   - (A) 10,000
   - (B) 24,000
   - (C) 33,000
   - (D) 10,800

2. Who was the sister of Lord Rama?
   - (A) Subhadra
   - (B) Shanta
   - (C) Yogmaya
   - (D) Ruma

3. Who was Goddess Sita in her previous birth?
   - (A) Bhargavi
   - (B) Satyabhama
   - (C) Vadavati
   - (D) Padmavati

4. Who killed Vidyutjiva?
   - (A) Ravana
   - (B) Hanuman
   - (C) Rama
   - (D) Bali

5. Who among the following cursed Ravana?
(A) Nalakuvara
(B) Vedavati
(C) Nandi
(D) All of These

6. Bharata was whose incarnation?
    (A) Panchajanya
    (B) Garuda
    (C) Kaumodaki
    (D) Kamdeva

7. Where did Rama meet Hanuman?
    (A) Kishkindha
    (B) Rishyamukh
    (C) Panchavati
    (D) Dandakaranya

8. Whose cry sounded like a thunder?
    (A) Dasharatha
    (B) Lakshmana
    (C) Sugreeva
    (D) Indrajit

9. Who narrated the story of the Ramayana to Garuda in the form of a crow?
(A) Hanuman
(B) Valmiki
(C) Kakabhushundi
(D) Jayanta

VI

Karna's Curse: A Battle Written in Blood; The Mahabharata Blood

In the sacred history of Hinduism, the Mahabharata stands as a monumental epic, both in scale and in spiritual significance. Comprising over 100,000 slokas and more than 1.8 million words, it is not merely a story—it is a mirror of human complexity, divine will, and the eternal struggle between dharma (righteousness) and adharma (unrighteousness).

Traditionally attributed to the sage Vyasa, the Mahabharata is not just an account of war between two families—the Kauravas and the Pandavas—but a profound philosophical, ethical, and emotional exploration of humanity's deepest dilemmas. Within its layered chapters, the epic addresses themes of duty, justice, destiny, identity, and sacrifice, while interweaving countless subplots, celestial interventions, and moral trials.

At its heart lies the Kurukshetra War, a cataclysmic eighteen-day battle that marks the end of an era and the beginning of a new one. But the war is not only external—it also symbolizes the inner war waged within each individual between loyalty and truth, love and loss, desire and duty.

Among the many complex characters who walk through this grand narrative, Karna shines with a tragic brilliance. Born to the unwed mother Kunti and the sun god Surya, Karna was abandoned at birth and raised by a charioteer's family. Though royal by blood, he lived as an outcast, condemned by society for his birth. Yet he rose to become one of the greatest warriors of his time, unmatched in archery, valor, and generosity.

Karna's life is marked by sacrifice, honor, and an unshakable commitment to his friend Duryodhana, even when that loyalty placed him on the wrong side of history. He was denied his true identity, insulted for his lineage, and constantly caught between fate and free will. His story reflects the harsh reality that righteousness is not always rewarded, and truth often walks a lonely path.

The Mahabharata presents Karna not merely as a warrior, but as a symbol of misunderstood nobility, of dharma struggling in a world clouded by karma. His tragic end is not a defeat, but a poignant reminder of how greatness can exist even in shadows.

Amidst gods, kings, sages, and warriors, the Mahabharata gives us the Bhagavad Gita, a divine discourse between Lord Krishna and Arjuna, in the middle of the battlefield. In this sacred dialogue, Krishna explains the essence of duty, detachment, and the immortal nature of the soul, guiding not just Arjuna, but all future generations toward the light of spiritual wisdom.

The Mahabharata is not just India's epic—it is India's conscience, echoing through time with timeless lessons. It teaches us that truth is not always black and white, and that heroism comes in many forms—sometimes even in blood-stained silence, like that of Karna.

QUIZ

1. How many verses Mahabharata has?
(A) 1,00,000
(B) 1,00,800
(C) 2,00,000
(D) 2,40,000

2. 'A' was slayed 'B', 'B' was slayed by 'C', 'C' was slayed by 'D',
'D' was slayed by 'E' and 'E' was slayed by 'F'.
'F' = Babruvahana, who was 'A'?
(A) Iravan
(B) Ghatotkacha
(C) Lakshman Kumar
(D) Vrishaketu

3. Name the conch shell of Bheema
(A) Sughosha
(B) Paundra
(C) Anantavijaya
(D) Hiranyagarbha

4. Who was Karna in his previous birth?
(A) Vrishasena
(B) Meghvarna
(C) Dambhodbhava
(D) Anjanaparvan

5. Whose bones did Shakuni use to make dice (for Chaucer)?
    (A) Subala
    (B) Alambusha
    (C) Kirmira
    (D) Viprachitti

৵

6. Who was the only Kaurava to fight from the Pandavas' side?
    (A) Vikarna
    (B) Yuyutsu
    (C) Chitrasena
    (D) Jalasandha

৵

7. Name the warrior who could finish the war in just one day?
    (A) Bhishma
    (B) Dronacharya
    (C) Karna
    (D) Barbarik

৵

8. Who killed Arjuna?
    (A) Kuvalyapeedha
    (B) Viparichitti
    (C) Satyaki
    (D) Babruvahana

৵

9. Who was married to Duryodhana's daughter, Lakshmana?
(A) Uluk
(B) Shyamkarna
(C) Aniruddha
(D) Sambha

VII

When God Walked the Earth

"Yada yada hi dharmasya glanir bhavati Bharata,
abhyutthanam adharmasya tadātmanaa srijāmyaham
Paritranaya sadhunam vinasaya cha duskritam dharma-
samsthapanarthaya sambhavami yuge yuge."
(Bhagavad Gita – Chapter 4, Verses 7–8)

This profound shloka, spoken by Lord Krishna in the Bhagavad Gita, encapsulates the eternal promise of the Divine. Translated, it means:

"O, Arjuna, O descendant of Bharata, whenever there is a decline in righteousness (dharma) and a rise in unrighteousness (adharma), I manifest Myself. I descend millennium after millennium to protect the virtuous, annihilate the wicked, and reestablish the principles of dharma."

According to this divine assurance, Lord Vishnu, the preserver of the universe, incarnates upon Earth whenever cosmic balance is disturbed. His descent—known as avatara—is not merely an event, but a divine intervention aimed at restoring harmony, guiding humanity, and eliminating evil.

As per the Srimad Bhagavatam (Bhagavata Purana), Lord Vishnu is said to have manifested in 24 principal incarnations, including the well-known Dashavatara—ten most celebrated forms. Each avatar carries a distinct purpose and symbolism, reflecting the infinite ways through which the Supreme Being engages with creation for its upliftment and protection.

QUIZ

1. Which form did Lord Vishnu take to restore and protect the Vedas from Madhu and Kaitabha?
    (A) Hayagriva
    (B) Varaha
    (C) Nar-Narayana
    (D) Kurma

ॐ

2. In which of the following incarnation, Lord Vishnu slayed Viradha?
    (A) Vamana
    (B) Matsya
    (C) Kalki
    (D)Rama

ॐ

3. Who among the following is the first incarnation of Lord Vishnu's dashavatara?
    (A) Mohini
    (B) Vyasa
    (C) Matsya
    (D) Kurma

ॐ

4. Which incarnation of Lord Vishnu was defeated by Sharabha avatar of Lord Shiva?
    (A) Vamana
    (B) Dattatreya
    (C) Narasimha
    (D) Parshurama

ॐ

5. Which incarnation of Lord Vishnu was present during the Mahabharata?
  (A) Krishna
  (B) Vyasa
  (C) Parshurama
  (D) All of These

ॐ

6. Which incarnation of Lord Vishnu was taught the skill of war by Lord Shiva?
  (A) Jay
  (B) Parshurama
  (C) Dhanavantari
  (D) Vijay

ॐ

7. Which incarnation of Lord Vishnu did penance of Lord Shiva at Kedarnath?
  (A) Nar-Narayana
  (B) Narada
  (C) Dattatreya
  (D) The Pandavas

ॐ

8. Which incarnation did Lord Vishnu take to slay demon king – Bali?
  (A) Mohini
  (B) Krishna
  (C) Vamana
  (D) Sanat Kumar

ॐ

9. Whose incarnation was Lord Vishnu's eighth avatar's mother?

    (A) Yogmaya

    (B) Vinata

    (C) Aditi

    (D) Kadru

VIII

Nine Goddesses, One Power

In the vast and vibrant tapestry of Hindu mythology, few deities embody both ferocity and grace, wrath and compassion, destruction and creation the way Goddess Durga does. Among her many forms, the Navadurga—the nine manifestations of Durga—stand out as a collective embodiment of her divine evolution during the sacred nine nights of Navaratri.

Worshipped with intense devotion across India and among Hindus worldwide, these nine goddesses are venerated as individual forces and as one united divine essence. Rooted deeply in the Shaktism and Shaivism sects, the Navadurga represent the cosmic journey of the Divine Mother in her battle against the mighty demon Mahishasura—a symbolic war between righteousness (dharma) and chaos (adharma).

According to Hindu scriptures, each of the nine days of Navaratri marks a distinct transformation of Goddess

Durga as she wages a relentless war to restore cosmic balance. These transitions are not merely mythological—they are spiritual metaphors reflecting the inner transformation of the devotee as they progress from discipline to strength, from inner struggle to spiritual awakening. On the tenth day, known as Vijayadashami or Dussehra, the victory of Durga is celebrated as the triumph of good over evil, of light over darkness.

Let us now meet the Nine Divine Shaktis of Navadurga:

- Shailaputri – Daughter of the Himalayas, she symbolizes strength, grounding, and the beginning of spiritual evolution.
- Brahmacharini – The radiant goddess of penance and discipline, she signifies austerity and the pursuit of wisdom.
- Chandraghanta – A warrior goddess with a crescent moon on her forehead, she epitomizes courage, grace, and the destruction of evil.
- Kushmanda – The creator of the universe, she is believed to have initiated cosmic existence with her divine smile.
- Skandamata – The nurturing mother of Lord Skanda (Kartikeya), she represents selfless love and motherly strength.
- Katyayani – Fierce and divine, she is the form of Durga who slayed Mahishasura, signifying justice and valor.
- Kalaratri – The most intense and fearsome aspect of the goddess, she destroys ignorance and removes darkness from all realms.
- Mahagauri – Radiant and serene, she embodies purity, transformation, and peace, calming all after the storm.
- Siddhidatri – The ultimate form of Durga, she bestows supernatural powers (siddhis) and spiritual fulfillment

to her devotees.

Each of these goddesses holds her own symbolism, energy, and purpose, yet together they form a powerful narrative arc—a journey of spiritual ascent, divine protection, and inner awakening. The Navadurga are not just deities to be worshipped—they are energies to be awakened within ourselves.

As we explore their divine stories, may we also reflect on our own battles, our inner demons, and the light that leads us toward truth, courage, and transformation.

QUIZ

1. Which is the fourth form of Goddess Durga?
(A) Mahagauri
(B) Brahmacharini
(C) Katyayni
(D) Kushmanda

ಞ

2. Name Parvati's lion vahana.
   (A) Dawon
   (B) Surapadman
   (C) Makara
   (D) Takshaka

ಞ

3. Which goddess is also known as Shubhankari?
   (A) Shailaputri
   (B) Siddhidatri
   (C) Kalaratri
   (D) Ambika

ಞ

4. Which goddess represents Veera rasa (Heroism)?
   (A) Sati
   (B) Skandamata
   (C) Katyayni
   (D) Mahakali

ಞ

5. Which of the following goddess is represented in white clothes?
   (A) Brahmacharini
   (B) Vaishnno Devi
   (C) Mahagauri
   (D) Both (A) and (C)

6. Which form of Goddess Durga has a third eye always open?
   (A) Chandraghanta
   (B) Skandamata
   (C) Shatakshi
   (D) Shakambhari

7. Which goddess killed Mahishasura?
   (A) Siddhidatri
   (B) Katyayni
   (C) Kalaratri
   (D) Mahalsa

8. Who was the father of Shailaputri?
   (A) Daksha
   (B) Shilad
   (C) Himavan
   (D) Sukarma

9. Which goddess represents wonders (Adbhuta rasa)?
(A) Chandraghanta
(B) Durga
(C) Siddhidatri
(D) Matsya

IX

Where Shiva Dwells: The Luminous Shrines

A Jyotirlinga is a radiant, sacred manifestation of Lord Shiva, worshipped across India as an infinite pillar of divine light. The term Jyotirlinga combines two Sanskrit words — Jyoti, meaning "light," and Linga, symbolizing the formless aspect of Shiva. These holy shrines are not merely stone idols, but are venerated as powerful cosmic centers where Shiva revealed himself in his most luminous and transcendental form.

According to a legendary episode in the Shiva Purana, a dispute once arose between Brahma, the creator, and Vishnu, the preserver, regarding who among them was the supreme deity. To resolve the conflict, Lord Shiva manifested as an endless pillar of light piercing the three realms — heaven, earth, and the underworld. Brahma took flight upon a swan to ascend the column, while Vishnu assumed the form of Varaha, the divine boar, and descended. Neither could find the beginning nor the end of the blazing light.

In an act of pride, Brahma falsely claimed he had reached the top and presented a Ketakī flower as evidence. Vishnu, however, humbly admitted defeat. Infuriated by Brahma's deceit, Shiva cursed him to never be worshipped in temples, while blessing Vishnu to be revered eternally for his truthfulness.

This divine pillar of light came to be known as the Jyotirlinga, signifying Shiva's limitless and formless nature. While the scriptures speak of 64 original Jyotirlingas, twelve are especially sacred and celebrated throughout India. These Dvādaśa Jyotirlingas are spread across the subcontinent, each bearing a unique name, legend, and energy, and are believed to be the epicenters of Lord Shiva's divine presence.

Each shrine is not only a spiritual beacon but also an architectural and cultural marvel, attracting millions of devotees and pilgrims year after year. Worshipping at the Jyotirlingas is believed to cleanse the soul, dissolve karmic burdens, and bring one closer to moksha — liberation from the cycle of birth and death.

QUIZ

1. Which was the first jyotirlinga?
(A) Kedarnath
(B) Somnath
(C) Omkareshwar
(D) Amarnath

2. Which jyotirlinga was established where Lord Shiva slayed Kumbhkarna's son?
(A) Bhimashankar
(B) Rameshwaram
(C) Mahakaaleshwar
(D) Baijnath

3. Which jyotirlinga is located in Verul?
(A) Trimbakeshwar
(B) Vishweshwara
(C) Grishneshwar
(D) Mahakaleshwar

4. Where is Omkareshwar jyotirlinga located?
(A) Ujjain
(B) Nasik
(C) Khandwa
(D) Varanasi

5. Which temple was built by the Pandavas after the Mahabharata war?
    (A) Nageshwar
    (B) Kalpeshwar
    (C) Rudranath
    (D) Kedarnath

৪৩

6. Which river is situated near Trimbakeshwar jyotirlinga?
    (A) Godavari
    (B) Tapti
    (C) Krishna
    (D) Sarayu

৪৩

7. Which jyotirlinga is associated with Lanka-King Ravana?
    (A) Rameshwaram
    (B) Baidyanath
    (C) Madhyamahesh
    (D) Tunganath

৪৩

8. Which jyotirlinga is located within 20kms from Dwarka?
    (A) Nageshwar
    (B) VIshwanath
    (C) Mallikaarjuna
    (D) Somnath

৪৩

9. Which jyotirlinga is situated on the side of the holy river 'Shipra'?
    (A) Kedarnath
    (B) Amarnath
    (C) Mahakaleshwar
    (D) Somnath

X

The Divine Assembly

In Hindu mythology, Devatas are divine beings who represent the subtle, spiritual forces behind all aspects of existence. While the terms Deva and Devata are often used interchangeably, Devatas are typically regarded as more specific or focused manifestations of divine power. They are both male and female, and each one governs a particular domain—ranging from natural elements to emotions, knowledge, actions, and even specific human activities.

Unlike the major gods of the Trimurti (Brahma, Vishnu, and Shiva) or the Tridevi (Saraswati, Lakshmi, and Parvati), Devtas function more as celestial administrators, ensuring the smooth functioning of the cosmos. They are personifications of energy and elements, present both in the outer universe and within our inner being. Every ritual in Hindu tradition often begins by invoking these Devtas—be it Agni Dev (Fire), Vayu Dev (Air), Surya Dev (Sun), or Chandra Dev (Moon).

The Devtas are worshipped through mantras, rituals, offerings, and prayers, not only to seek blessings but to acknowledge the divine presence in all walks of life. They remind us that the divine is not distant or separate, but inherently woven into the fabric of our daily experience.

As we explore the concept of Devtas, we begin to understand that spirituality in Hinduism is not limited to grand temples or complex philosophies—it is also found in the act of lighting a lamp, cooking a meal, reading a book, or showing kindness. Every action becomes sacred when we recognize the Devata within it.

QUIZ

1. Name the ancestor of the Pandavas who replaced Indra as the king of Heaven for some time.
   (A) Dushyanta
   (B) Nahusha
   (C) Bharata
   (D) None of These

2. Who cursed the Moon God?
   (A) Daksha
   (B) Ganesha
   (C) Durvasa
   (D) Both (A) and (B)

3. Who was the son of Surya deva?
   (A) Shani
   (B) Karna
   (C) Sugriva
   (D) All of These

4. Crocodile/Makara is the vahana of which devata?
   (A) Varuna
   (B) Vayu
   (C) Agni
   (D) None of These

5. Which devata was born as the son of Lord Krishna and Rukmini?
    (A) Ashwini
    (B) Chandra
    (C) Kama
    (D) Indra

ॐ

6. Who among the following was the son of Vayu deva?
    (A) Shakuni
    (B) Bheema
    (C) Yuyutsu
    (D) Dhritarashtra

ॐ

7. Which demon was killed by Indra from behind?
    (A) Vritrasur
    (B) Sumali
    (C) Tarakasur
    (D) Vajrang

ॐ

8. Who among the following is the mother of Surya's charioteer?
    (A) Kadru
    (B) Revati
    (C) Vinata
    (D) Aditi

ॐ

9. Who was the commander-in-chief of the devatas' army?

(A) Ganesha
(B) Varuna
(C) Nahusha
(D) Skanda

XI
Lords of Ego and Ambition

In the vast pantheon of Indic mythology, the Asuras represent a fascinating and complex class of beings—powerful, ambitious, and often misunderstood. Traditionally depicted as power-seeking entities, the Asuras are considered to be closely related to the more benevolent Devas, though frequently positioned in opposition to them. This duality forms the foundation of many cosmic battles and philosophical metaphors in Hindu thought.

According to the ancient Hindu scriptures, the Asuras and Devas are locked in an eternal struggle, symbolizing the timeless conflict between righteousness and ego, light and shadow, order and chaos. While Devas are often associated with harmony and divine purpose, Asuras are portrayed as beings whose aspirations for power and dominance lead them away from dharma (righteousness). Yet, it is important to note that not all Asuras are purely malevolent; some display admirable traits such as loyalty, strength, wisdom, and even devotion, adding layers of moral complexity to their stories.

In many scriptures and cosmological theories, Asuras are described as superhuman demigods—intensely powerful and deeply influential within the mythic universe. Their rivalry with the Devas is not just a physical battle, but a symbolic one, representing the inner conflict that exists within every being: the tug of higher virtues versus lower desires, the sacred versus the self-centered.

Asuras, along with Devas, Yakshas, Rakshasas, Gandharvas, Apsaras, and other celestial or semi-divine entities, populate the rich and diverse mythological fabric of Hinduism. From Hiranyakashipu and Ravana to Mahishasura and Vritra, these figures stand not only as antagonists but also as spiritual metaphors, teaching valuable lessons about pride, penance, redemption, and the eternal law of karma.

Their tales, while often painted in shades of conflict and destruction, ultimately contribute to the cosmic balance, reminding us that the path to enlightenment is forged not only through divine grace but also through the trials of temptation, ego, and inner darkness.

QUIZ

1. Which demon got the boon to be killed by Lord Shiva's son?
    (A) Tare
    (B) Vajrang
    (C) Vidyunmali
    (D) Tarakasura

ॐ

2. Who among the following was the brother of Putana?
    (A) Kansa
    (B) Bakasura
    (C) Aghasura
    (D) Both (B) and (C)

ॐ

3. Shishupal is his previous birth was?
    (A) Viradha
    (B) Ravana
    (C) Kumbhakarna
    (D) Kabandha

ॐ

4. Hiranyaksha was reborn as?
    (A) Jay
    (B) Vijay
    (C) Kumbhakarna
    (D) Makaradhwaja

ॐ

5. Which demoness cursed Lord Vishnu?
(A) Vrinda
(B) Daruka
(C) Kaikasi
(D) Chhayagrahini

॰

6. Who was the father of Makardhwaja?
    (A) Yama
    (B) Hanuman
    (C) Bali
    (D) Indrajit

॰

7. Which demon was blessed with a boon that only the goddess could kill him?
    (A) Mahishasura
    (B) Shumbha
    (C) Munda
    (D) All of These

॰

8. Which demon was cursed by Ashok Sundari?
    (A) Hunda
    (B) Kaitabha
    (C) Nishumbha
    (D) Dhenukasura

॰

9. Which demons' daughter married Lord Krishna's grandson?
(A) Keshi
(B) Arunasura
(C) Banasura
(D) Vyomasura

XII

Sacred Minds, Silent Power: The Ancient Sages

The term sage refers to a spiritually accomplished and enlightened Brahmin—an individual who has transcended the ordinary to attain supreme wisdom and insight. Sages, or Rishis, occupy a revered space in the tapestry of Hindu mythology, frequently appearing in the ancient Vedic texts as the original seers (mantradrashta) who received divine knowledge through deep spiritual intuition.

These venerable beings are believed to have composed the sacred hymns of the Vedas, not through intellectual pursuit alone, but through profound meditative experience. The sounds of these mantras were not invented—they were heard, or revealed, during states of intense tapas (austerity and penance), making the sages mere instruments through which cosmic truths flowed.

In post-Vedic Hindu tradition, Rishis are honored as great yogis who, through unwavering discipline and inner stillness, realized the eternal truths of the universe. Their insights form the very bedrock of Sanatan Dharma, influencing not only religious rituals but also philosophy, ethics, and metaphysics.

From Maharishi Vashishtha and Vishwamitra to Atri, Bhrigu, and Agastya, the Rishis represent a lineage of enlightened thought that continues to inspire seekers of knowledge and spirituality. They are more than historical or mythological figures—they are guiding lights, whose legacy continues to illuminate the path of Dharma, devotion, and divine realization.

QUIZ

1. Who was the daughter of Sage Vishwamitra?
(A) Shakuntala
(B) Khyati
(C) Vijaya
(D) Shanta

ॐ

2. Who is the Father of Astrology in India?
(A) Gautama
(B) Agastya
(C) Bhrigu
(D) Vashishtha

ॐ

3. Who adopted Shakuntala?
(A) Vishwamitra
(B) Durvasa
(C) Kanava
(D) Bharadwaja

ॐ

4. Who cursed Lord Shiva?
(A) Daksha
(B) Kashyapa
(C) Durvasa
(D) All of These

ॐ

5. Who was the father of Sage Vyasa?
(A) Atri
(B) Parashara
(C) Valmiki
(D) Markandeya

6. Which sage was the grandfather of Ravana?
    (A) Pulastya
    (B) Parshurama
    (C) Vishrava
    (D) Shukracharya

7. Which sage cursed Karna?
    (A) Durvasa
    (B) Kripacharya
    (C) Parshurama
    (D) Dronacharya

8. Which sage wrote the Mahamrityunjaya mantra?
    (A) Veda Vyasa
    (B) Markandeya
    (C) Brihaspati
    (D) Vashishtha

9. Who among the following is one of these ashta chiranjivi (the eight immortals)?
(A) Veda Vyada
(B) Kripacharya
(C) Parshurama
(D) All of These

Answer Key

QUIZ -1: *Ganesha & His Siblings*

1. (A) Mallikaarjuna: According to the Purans, it is believed that Lord Shiva and Goddess Parvati could not make up their minds as to which of their sons, should get married first. To determine who would be first, they set a contest for the two: Whoever would go around the world first would be the winner. Ganesha outwitted his brother, Skanda and won the race. When Skanda heard about this on his return, he was upset. He left for Mount Krounch, and started living there. His parents visited him there and hence there is a shrine for both there – A linga for Shiva and a Shakti Peetha for Parvati.

2. (B) Ashoka Sundari: Ashok Sundari is the elder sister of Ganesha and the younger one of Kartikeya. She was born by worshipping Kalpavriksha.

3. (B) Mahabharata: When Sage Vyasa decided to compose the epic Mahabharata, he sought someone capable of writing it down without error. He chose Lord Ganesha, known for his intellect and wisdom. Ganesha agreed to write the epic, but under the condition that Vyasa would recite it without pause. In turn, Vyasa required that Ganesha must understand each verse before writing it.

As Vyasa dictated, Ganesha wrote with unmatched speed, using his broken tusk as a pen. Vyasa, to maintain pace, would occasionally recite complex verses that gave him time to compose the next sections. Through this divine partnership, the Mahabharata was created—an enduring symbol of devotion, intellect, and spiritual wisdom.

৺

4. (B) Kalpavriksha: Ashok Sundari, the daughter of Lord Shiva and Goddess Parvati, was created from a wish. One day, Parvati felt lonely in the absence of her son Kartikeya and wished for a daughter to ease her sorrow. From the divine Kalpavriksha tree, a celestial girl was born—beautiful and radiant. She was named Ashok Sundari, meaning "the beautiful one who removes sorrow." Loved dearly by her parents, she later married King Nahusha and played a lesser-known yet divine role in Hindu mythology.

৺

5. (D) Shukracharya: Shukracharya, the revered guru of the Asuras, was known for his immense knowledge and mastery of powerful mantras. When Jalandhar, a mighty demon born from Lord Shiva's fury, rose to power, he was guided and mentored by Shukracharya. Under his tutelage, Jalandhar learned the secrets of warfare, strategy, and divine knowledge, becoming nearly invincible. With Shukracharya's wisdom and blessings, Jalandhar challenged the Devas and ruled over the heavens for a time, until he was ultimately defeated by Lord Shiva himself.

৺

6. (A) Andhaka: Goddess Parvati once playfully covered Lord Shiva's eyes while they were enjoying a game of chausar (dice) on Mount Kailash. Though just for a moment, the universe was plunged into complete darkness, as Shiva's eyes are the source of light and life. From this sudden darkness and the intense heat of Shiva's closed third eye, a drop of sweat fell to the earth and took form.

This drop gave birth to a child—blind and born in total darkness—who came to be known as Andhaka, meaning "born of darkness." The child was later adopted by the demon king Hiranyaksha and grew up among the Asuras, unaware of his divine origin.

৵

7. (C) Lohitang: Lohitang was born from a drop of Lord Shiva's sweat during the fierce and cosmic dance of Tandava. When Lord Shiva performed the Tandava in intense rage and divine energy, the power of his movements shook the cosmos. As his fury surged, a single drop of his sweat fell to the ground.

From that powerful drop emerged Lohitang, a being infused with heat, strength, and a reddish glow—hence the name "Lohitang" (meaning "red-bodied" or "fiery one"). Though born from Shiva himself, Lohitang later came to oppose the Devas and took a place among the powerful Asuras

৵

8. (C) Nahusha; Kuruvansh: Ashok Sundari, the daughter of Lord Shiva and Goddess Parvati, was born from the divine Kalpavriksha to ease Parvati's loneliness. As she grew up, it was foretold that she would marry Nahusha, a brave and noble prince destined to become a powerful king. According to legend, Ashok Sundari once encountered the demon Hunda, who desired her. She refused his advances and declared her loyalty to Nahusha. Angered, Hunda tried to harm Nahusha, but with the blessings of Shiva and Parvati, Nahusha defeated the demon in battle. In time, Ashok Sundari and Nahusha were united in marriage. Nahusha later went on to rule the heavens temporarily as king of the Devas, fulfilling the prophecy of their divine union.

ॐ

9. (B) Sakha, Visakha: According to some folk traditions, after Kartikeya (Murugan) married Devasena and Valli, he was blessed with two divine sons—Sakha and Vishakha. These sons were believed to be born to assist in Kartikeya's divine duties, especially in the protection of righteousness (dharma) and the defeat of evil forces.

Sakha and Vishakha were said to be born from the divine energy of Kartikeya after a great yagna (fire ritual) performed by the gods, requesting aid in the constant battle against rising demonic powers. Kartikeya, though often revered as celibate in many traditions, was seen here in his householder form, continuing the lineage of divine warriors.

Raised with the blessings of both their mothers and divine sages, Sakha and Vishakha inherited their father's valor, wisdom, and devotion, and were believed to assist him in his campaigns to restore balance in the world.

QUIZ - 2: *The Divine Forces of Creation & Knowledge*

1. (C) Lord Shiva: Once, Brahma, the creator god, had five heads and became arrogant, believing himself to be the supreme creator. One of his heads began to lust after Saraswati, his own daughter, which was considered inappropriate. Disturbed by Brahma's ego and misconduct, Lord Shiva appeared and cut off Brahma's fifth head.

This act symbolized the destruction of ego and false pride. After this, Brahma was humbled and became more devoted, while Shiva's act reinforced the principle that even gods must uphold righteousness and humility.

॰

2. (B) Padmakshi: Padmakshi is one of the revered forms of Goddess Saraswati, whose name means "She with lotus-shaped eyes" (Padma = lotus, Akshi = eyes). This form symbolizes purity, wisdom, and serene beauty.

According to legend, after the creation of the universe, Saraswati took the form of Padmakshi to bestow knowledge and enlightenment upon the world. Her lotus-like eyes represent spiritual awakening and the ability to see beyond the material realm.

Worshipped especially in South India, Padmakshi embodies the divine power of speech, learning, and arts, inspiring devotees to pursue wisdom with clarity and devotion.

॰

3. (D) Kartik Purnima: Kartik Purnima, the full moon day of the Hindu month Kartik, is considered highly auspicious.

According to legend, it is the day when Lord Brahma performed a great yajna (sacred ritual) at Pushkar in Rajasthan. This was the only time and place where Lord Brahma is said to have been worshipped on earth.

To mark this divine event, a sacred lake was created at Pushkar, and a grand temple was built there in his honor. Hence, devotees worship Lord Brahma on Kartik Purnima, especially at Pushkar, seeking blessings of creation, purity, and spiritual awakening.

౸

4.(D) Both (A) and (C): Lord Brahma and Goddess Saraswati had many sons which included both Chitragupta (Yama's assistant) and Prajapati Daksha.Lord Brahma and Goddess Saraswati had many sons which included both Chitragupta (Yama's assistant) and Prajapati Daksha.

౸

5. (A) Swan: Goddess Saraswati, the embodiment of knowledge, wisdom, and arts, is traditionally depicted riding a swan (Hamsa) or sometimes a peacock. The swan is her primary vahana, symbolizing purity, discernment, and spiritual grace.

౸

6. (C) Pushkar: Pushkar, a sacred town in Rajasthan, is home to the world's rarest and most famous temple dedicated to Lord Brahma, the creator god. According to legend, Brahma chose Pushkar to perform a grand yajna (sacred fire ritual) to seek blessings for creation and the universe's well-being.

During the yajna, a lotus flower fell from Brahma's hand onto the earth, and a holy lake, called Pushkar Lake, emerged at that spot. It is believed that bathing in this lake on Kartik Purnima, the full moon day in the month of Kartik, washes away sins and grants liberation.

Because Brahma's worship is rare and his temples few, Pushkar holds immense spiritual significance, attracting devotees who seek the blessings of creation, wisdom, and divine grace from Lord Brahma himself.

7. (B) Basara: After the Mahabharata war, sage Vyasa and his disciples looked for a peaceful place to meditate. They arrived at Dandakaarnya. Later, a king of Karnataka built the Saraswati temple here and this place came to be known as Basara.

8. (A) Lord Vishnu: Lord Brahma mediates upon Lord Vishnu while Lord Vishnu meditates upon Lord Shiva.

9. (D) Basant Panchami: Basant Panchami signals the renewal of life, creativity, and intellect. Since Saraswati represents knowledge and wisdom, she is invoked to bless students, scholars, artists, and seekers with clarity and learning.

QUIZ - 3: *Guardians of Prosperity and Preservation*

1. (B) 24: According to the Bhagavata Purana (Shrimad Bhagavatam), Lord Vishnu is said to have 24 principal avatars (incarnations), though he is believed to have countless manifestations. These avatars descend to restore dharma, protect devotees, and destroy evil.

※

2. (A) Owl: Goddess Lakshmi's owl is not just a symbolic vehicle but a moral reminder—to stay grounded, wise, and vigilant even while enjoying material abundance. It teaches that true prosperity comes with insight, balance, and inner light, not just external wealth.

※

3. (B) Panchajanya: According to the Mahabharata and Vishnu Purana, the conch Panchajanya came into Lord Vishnu's possession after he vanquished a demon named Panchajana, who had taken the form of a sea creature and lived in the deep ocean. This demon had once taken a Brahmin boy (the son of Vishnu's guru), and Vishnu, in his avatar as Krishna, entered the ocean, killed Panchajana, and retrieved the conch shell from his body.

※

4. (D) Sharad Purnima: Sharad Purnima, the full moon night marking the end of the monsoon and the beginning of harvest season, is closely associated with the worship of Goddess Lakshmi, the deity of wealth and prosperity.

According to Hindu mythology, it is believed that on the night of Sharad Purnima, Goddess Lakshmi descends to Earth, moving from house to house, blessing those who are awake, clean, and engaged in prayer or spiritual activities with wealth, happiness, and success. It is said she favours industrious and disciplined households and avoids places that are dirty or filled with laziness.

People stay awake all night in devotion, keeping their homes well-lit and pure, in hopes of inviting the Goddess of Fortune. This night is also believed to be the time when the moon showers nectar (amrit), and kheer (sweet rice pudding) is traditionally placed under the moonlight and then consumed as blessed food.

Thus, Sharad Purnima is revered as a night of divine grace, abundance, and celestial blessings, with Lakshmi as the central divine figure of worship.

ॐ

5. (A) Shiva: According to Linga Puran, Lord Shiva gave Vishnu his weapon, the Sudarshan Chakra.

ॐ

6. (D) Vrinda: Vrinda, a pious and devoted wife of the asura king Jalandhar, was known for her unwavering chastity and devotion, which gave her husband immense power. Even the gods could not defeat Jalandhar as long as Vrinda remained loyal and pure.

To break this protection, Lord Vishnu took the form of Jalandhar and tricked Vrinda, breaking her chastity. As a result, Jalandhar was defeated by Lord Shiva in battle.

Realizing she had been deceived, a heartbroken and enraged Vrinda cursed Lord Vishnu that he too would suffer the pain of separation from his beloved. This curse is believed to have manifested in Rama's exile and separation from Sita in the Ramayana.

Afterward, Vrinda immolated herself in sorrow, and from her ashes, the Tulsi plant was born — now considered sacred and a symbol of pure devotion in Hinduism.

❦

7. (A) Bhargavi: Goddess Lakshmi is called Bhargavi because she is believed to be the daughter of Sage Bhrigu, one of the revered Saptarishis (seven great sages) in Hindu mythology.

❦

8. (C) Srinivas: When Sage Bhrigu kicked Lord Vishnu on his chest, Goddess Lakshmi felt humiliated and thus left Vaikuntha and descended on Earth. To bring his consort back, Lord Vishnu incarnated on this Earth as Srinivas and is worshipped as Lord Tirupati Balaji.

❦

9. (D) Both (A) and (B): In Hindu mythology, Harihara (also called Shankaranarayana) is the divine fusion of Lord Vishnu (Hari) and Lord Shiva (Hara), symbolizing the unity and harmony of these two major deities, who are sometimes worshipped separately but are ultimately one and the same supreme reality.

QUIZ - 4: *Shiva-Shakti: The Cosmic Union*

1. (D) 12: According to the Shiva Purana, Lord Shiva originally manifested in 64 Jyotirlingas across the Indian subcontinent. However, 12 of them came to be regarded as the most powerful and spiritually significant, due to their deep-rooted mythology, intense devotional worship, and the miracles associated with them.

2. (B) Kali: Raktabija was a powerful demon who had received a terrifying boon: every drop of his blood that touched the ground would give rise to a new clone of himself. During the fierce battle between the Devas and the demon army led by Shumbha and Nishumbha, Raktabija stepped in, and none of the gods or goddesses could defeat him due to his regenerative power.

To end his tyranny, Goddess Kali emerged from the forehead of Goddess Durga in a form of pure, unstoppable rage. As she fought Raktabija, Kali spread her enormous tongue and drank all his blood before it could fall to the ground, preventing new demons from forming. She then devoured all the Raktabija clones, eventually killing him and ending his reign of terror.

3. (A) Kashyapa: Once, Surya, the sun god, became arrogant about his brilliance and powers, letting pride cloud his judgment. His radiance grew unbearable, disrupting cosmic balance. Lord Shiva, in a moment of divine intervention, beheaded Surya to humble him and restore order.

Enraged by this act, Kashyap Rishi, Surya's father and one of the revered Saptarishis, cursed Lord Shiva in grief and fury. He declared: "Just as my son lost his head, so too shall your son be fated to lose his own."

This curse eventually manifested in the beheading of Shiva's son, Ganesha, years later — fulfilling Kashyap's words and intertwining divine actions with karmic consequences.

&

4. (C) Rati: After Kamadeva, the god of love, tried to disrupt Lord Shiva's meditation to make him fall in love with Parvati, Shiva opened his third eye and burned Kamadeva to ashes.

Grief-stricken by her husband's sudden death, Rati, Kamadeva's wife, was devastated. Overwhelmed by sorrow and anger, she blamed Parvati for Kamadeva's demise, believing it was her desire that led to the attempt, and eventually cursed her of infertility.

&

5. (B) Jalandhar: According to legend, Jalandhar was born from the flames of Lord Shiva's third eye when he opened it in a moment of divine fury. As Shiva's energy merged with the vast ocean, a powerful child emerged from the waters. The ocean god, Varuna, raised the child and named him Jalandhar, meaning "born of the water" (Jal = water, andhar = within).

Blessed with immense strength and beauty, Jalandhar grew to become a formidable asura (demon) king. Because he originated from Shiva's energy, he possessed divine powers and was nearly invincible. His birth would later set the stage for a cosmic battle between him and the gods, especially Shiva, whom he once challenged in arrogance.

6. (D) Mahalsa: According to legend, the demon brothers Malla and Mani had gained immense power and were tormenting the gods and devotees. The devas prayed to Goddess Parvati to intervene and save the world from their tyranny.

In response, Parvati took the form of Mahalsa, a fierce and radiant warrior goddess. She was born to a devout couple in the village of Verna in Goa. As Mahalsa grew up, her divine nature became evident—she possessed immense strength, wisdom, and beauty.

When the time came, Mahalsa went to battle against Malla and Mani. She slayed Malla in a fierce fight, restoring balance to the world. Mani, however, repented for his actions. Moved by his surrender, Mahalsa spared his life and made him her Dwarpalaka (gatekeeper).

Mahalsa is worshipped widely in Goa and Maharashtra, especially as the Kuladevi (family deity) of many communities.

7. (A) Kadru: Kadru is one of the wives of the sage Kashyapa and the mother of the Nāgas (serpent beings), including Vasuki, Shesha, and Takshaka. According to the Puranas, Kadru gave birth to a thousand powerful serpents, and Vasuki was among the most prominent.

Vasuki later became a devoted follower of Lord Shiva, who honored him by wearing him around his neck, symbolizing control over the primal energies and fearlessness in the face of death.

8. (D) Both (B) and (C): Lord Hanuman is considered a Rudra avatar of Lord Shiva, born to aid Lord Rama (an avatar of Vishnu) during the Treta Yuga. He symbolizes strength, devotion, and selfless service, and is deeply revered in Hindu tradition.

Ashwatthama, the son of Dronacharya, is also believed to be a partial incarnation of Shiva. Endowed with immense power and immortality, he played a crucial role in the Mahabharata. However, due to his violent actions after the war, he was cursed by Krishna to live forever in suffering and isolation.

Both are immortal and represent different aspects of Lord Shiva—Hanuman as devotion and protection, Ashwatthama as wrath and consequence.

ॐ

9. (C) 52: Sati, the daughter of King Daksha and the first consort of Lord Shiva, married Shiva against her father's wishes. Later, Daksha organized a grand yagna (sacrificial ritual) but did not invite Shiva and Sati. Insulted and heartbroken by the disrespect shown to her husband, Sati immolated herself in the sacrificial fire.

When Lord Shiva learned of Sati's death, he was overcome with grief and fury. He lifted Sati's lifeless body and began performing the Tandava, the dance of destruction. To stop the impending cosmic destruction, Lord Vishnu used his Sudarshan Chakra to cut Sati's body into pieces.

These pieces fell across different places in the Indian subcontinent, and wherever a part of her body fell, that site became a Shakti Peetha—a revered shrine of the Divine Feminine.

QUIZ - 5: Rama's Journey: The Eternal Ideal

1. (B) 24,000: The Valmiki Ramayana, composed by the sage Maharishi Valmiki, is one of the two great Sanskrit epics of ancient India (the other being the Mahabharata). It is said to consist of approximately 24,000 shlokas (verses), divided into seven kandas (books):

- Bala Kanda – The childhood of Rama
- Ayodhya Kanda – Events in Ayodhya before Rama's exile
- Aranya Kanda – Rama's life in the forest
- Kishkindha Kanda – Rama's meeting with Hanuman and Sugriva
- Sundara Kanda – Hanuman's journey to Lanka
- Yuddha Kanda – The war with Ravana
- Uttara Kanda – Rama's return and final years (considered a later addition by some scholars)

The number 24,000 is also significant symbolically—many believe Valmiki composed one verse for each breath of a human being in a day, reflecting Rama as the essence of life itself.

৪৩

2. (B) Shanta: Shanta, the lesser-known elder sister of Lord Rama, has a fascinating and often overlooked story in the Ramayana tradition.

Shanta was the adopted daughter of King Romapada of Anga, but she was actually born to King Dasharatha and Queen Kaushalya, making her the eldest sibling of Rama, Lakshmana, Bharata, and Shatrughna.

Dasharatha and Kaushalya, desiring to strengthen political alliances and also fulfill Romapada's wish for a child, gave Shanta in adoption to the childless Romapada and his queen Varshini. She grew up as the princess of Anga and was raised with love and royal care.

Shanta was known to be wise, graceful, and highly learned. She married Rishi Rishyasringa, a sage of great spiritual power, who had grown up in isolation without any knowledge of worldly life.

੪

3. (C) Vedavati: In her previous birth, Sita is believed to have been Vedavati, a woman deeply devoted to Lord Vishnu and determined to marry him.

Vedavati was the daughter of a sage named Bhrigu. She lived a life of austerity and penance in the forest, praying fervently to Lord Vishnu to accept her as his consort. One day, Ravana, the king of Lanka, saw her and was captivated by her beauty. When she rejected his advances, he tried to violate her.

To protect her chastity, Vedavati immolated herself in fire, vowing to be reborn to become the cause of Ravana's destruction.

In her next life, she was born as Sita, the daughter of King Janaka, and became the wife of Lord Rama (an incarnation of Vishnu). It was through her abduction by Ravana that the chain of events in the Ramayana unfolded, eventually leading to Ravana's death.

Thus, Vedavati's vow was fulfilled, and justice prevailed.

੪

4. (A) Ravana: When Shurpanakha grew up, she secretly married the Danava prince of the Kalkeya Danava clan,

Vidyutjihva. Ravana became enraged with Shurpanakha for marrying a Danava. The Danavas were the mortal enemies of Rakshasas. Enraged Ravana decided to kill both of them. Thus waged a war against Vidyutjihva's army and killed him in a battle. Ravana was about to kill Surpanakha too but Ravana's wife Mandodari saved her. Ravana's brothers Kumbhakarna and Vibhishana also appealed to him to spare Surpanakha's life.

Mandodari asked Surpanakha to roam and search for another husband. Shurpanakha then split her time between Lanka and the woods of Southern India, sometimes living with her forest-dwelling Asura relatives, Khara and Dushana, on Ravana's orders.

৯৩

5. (D) All of These: The three major curses on Ravana:

1. Nandi's Curse:

When Ravana tried to lift Mount Kailash to display his strength, Lord Shiva pinned him under it. Nandi, Shiva's gatekeeper, mocked Ravana's arrogance. In retaliation, Ravana insulted Nandi's monkey-like form. Enraged, Nandi cursed Ravana that monkeys would one day become the cause of his destruction — which came true through Lord Rama's vanara army.

2. Vedavati's Curse:

Vedavati was a devoted woman meditating to marry Lord Vishnu. Ravana, enchanted by her beauty, tried to violate her. She resisted and self-immolated to protect her honor. Before dying, she cursed Ravana that she would be reborn to destroy him — she was later reborn as Sita, whose abduction led to his downfall.

3. Nalakuvara's Curse:

Ravana once violated Rambha, an apsara who was the wife of Nalakuvara (Kubera's son). Enraged, Nalakuvara cursed Ravana that if he ever tried to force himself on a woman again, his head would shatter into pieces. This curse prevented him from harming Sita during her captivity in Lanka.

These curses played a vital role in shaping Ravana's destiny and eventual defeat.

6. (C) Panchajanya:

Bharata, the younger brother of Lord Rama, is considered to be the incarnation (avatar) of Panchajanya Shankha, the divine conch shell of Lord Vishnu.

Bharata, as the avatar of Shankha, represents the divine call to dharma. His unwavering devotion to Lord Rama, refusal to take the throne, and his rule as Rama's regent with Rama's sandals on the throne reflect the humility and spiritual power associated with the Shankha.

7. (B) Rishyamukha: After Sita was abducted by Ravana, Lord Rama and Lakshmana wandered through the forests in search of her. Their journey brought them near Rishyamukh Mountain, where the exiled monkey king Sugriva was hiding, fearing his brother Vali.

Sugriva, upon seeing the two princes, grew suspicious and sent his trusted minister Hanuman in disguise to learn who they were. Hanuman approached Rama and Lakshmana in the form of a humble ascetic. But upon hearing Rama speak and sensing his divine presence, Hanuman immediately revealed his true form.

Deeply moved by Rama's nobility, Hanuman offered to help and led them to Sugriva. This meeting marked the beginning of a divine friendship. It was at Rishyamukh that Rama and Hanuman first met, a moment that would shape the course of the Ramayana and form a bond of eternal devotion

ॐ

8. (D) Indrajit: When Indrajit (Meghnad), the mighty son of Ravana, was born, his first cry was so powerful and thunderous that it resembled a storm rumbling across the sky. This mighty roar was said to foretell the strength and valor he would display as a fierce warrior in the great battles to come. From the moment of his birth, Meghnad's presence was marked by an extraordinary power that echoed like thunder throughout the heavens.

ॐ

9. (C) Kakabhushundi: Kakabhushundi, after being cursed to be a crow, but originally just Bhushundi, is a sage featured in Hindu literature. He is one of the characters of the Ramacaritamanasa, an Awadhi poem about the deity Rama by the saint Tulsidas. He is also known as Kaaga Pujandar in Tamil culture.

Kakabhushundi is depicted as a devotee of Rama, who narrates the story of the Ramayana to Garuda in the form of a crow.

QUIZ - 6: Karna's Curse: A Battle Written in Blood; The Mahabharata Blood

1. (A) 1,00,000: The Mahabharata is renowned as the longest epic poem ever written, containing about 100,000 shlokas (verses), which amounts to over 200,000 individual lines of poetry. This immense length makes it roughly ten times the size of the Iliad and Odyssey combined, highlighting its vast scope and significance in Hindu mythology and literature.

2. (A) Iravan: Given that 'F' = Babruvahana who killed 'E"

Babruvahana was the son of Arjuna and Chitrangada, the princess of Manipur. Unaware of their relationship, Babruvahana grew up to be a strong and skilled warrior. During the Ashwamedha Yagna, Arjuna's horse wandered into Manipur, and Babruvahana confronted his father in battle. A fierce fight ensued, and Babruvahana defeated Arjuna, even killing him. Later, realizing Arjuna was his father, Babruvahana was devastated.

Therefore, 'E' = Arjuna.

During the great Kurukshetra war in the Mahabharata, Arjuna and Karna faced each other in a fierce battle. Karna, the formidable warrior and rival of Arjuna, was the son of Kunti but fought for the Kauravas. In their final encounter, Karna, one of the greatest warriors of the Mahabharata and known for his unmatched valor and generosity, fought fiercely on the Kaurava side. His skill and courage shone throughout the battle. However, during their final duel in the Kurukshetra war, Karna's chariot wheel got stuck in the mud. Seizing this rare moment, Arjuna, guided by Krishna, struck the fatal arrow, ending the life of this legendary hero and changing the course of the war forever.

Thus, 'D' = Karna.

While the fierce Kurukshetra war, Ghatotkacha—Bhima's mighty son—used his magical powers to terrorize the Kaurava army at night. His immense strength and illusions caused great damage, forcing the Kauravas into desperation. To stop him, Karna unleashed his divine weapon, the powerful Vasavi Shakti, granted by Indra, which he had been saving for Arjuna. With this formidable weapon, Karna struck down Ghatotkacha, sacrificing his most potent boon to protect the Kauravas and turn the tide of battle.

Hence, 'C' = Ghatotkacha.

Alambusha was a Rakshasa demon in the Mahabharata who fought on the Kaurava side during the Kurukshetra War. He was a powerful demon who joined the Kauravas, seeking revenge for his brother Bakasur's death at the hands of Bhima. During the Night war on the fourteenth day of the war. Alambusha was killed by Ghatotkacha.

So, 'B' = Alambusha

Alambusha is primarily known for killing Arjuna's son Iravan. Iravan also known as Iravat and Iravant, is a minor character from the Hindu epic Mahabharata. The son of Pandava prince Arjuna and the Naga princess Ulupi (daughter of serpent Vasuki). Iravan was wreaking havoc on the Kaurava army, leading Duryodhana to summon Alambusha to confront him. They engaged in a fierce battle, with both using their magical powers. Iravan was ultimately killed by Alambusha, who struck him with his sword.

Therefore, 'A' = Iravan.

3. (B) Paundra: Bhima, the second of the Pandava brothers, used a conch shell named Paundra. This conch, like those of other warriors, was used to announce the start of battle or to signal important events. Bhima's Paundra conch was known for its powerful, resounding sound, signifying his strength and ferocity on the battlefield.

૪૭

4. (C) Dambhodbhava: In his previous life, Karna was an asura named Dambhodbhava, or sometimes Sahasrakavacha, who had received a boon from the Sun God (Surya) granting him a thousand invulnerable armors. This boon allowed him to control the universe, causing fear and terror. The divine sages Nara-Narayana fought with him, destroying 99 armors before Dambhodbhava sought refuge with Surya, who protected him from being destroyed. Surya then conceived Kunti with the demon, and Karna was born with the remaining armor and earrings.

૪૭

5. (A) Subala: King Subala of Gandhara and his family were imprisoned by the Kauravas in Hastinapur. Bhishma had captured the royal family. With no food or water, they slowly began dying in captivity.

To ensure at least one member survived to take revenge, Subala and his sons chose Shakuni to be fed the little food they had. Before dying, Subala asked that Shakuni always remember the cruelty done to their family.

After his death, Shakuni crafted dice from his father's thigh bones. These dice were no ordinary ones—they were enchanted, always obeying Shakuni's will. He later used these very dice to defeat the Pandavas in the infamous game of dice, setting the stage for the Mahabharata war and fulfilling his vow of revenge.

৪০

6. (B) Yuyutsu: Yuyutsu was the son of Dhritarashtra and a Vaishya (maid) woman, making him a half-brother to the Kauravas. Unlike his brothers, Yuyutsu was righteous and just. On the eve of the Kurukshetra war, he defected from the Kaurava camp and joined the Pandavas, unable to support Duryodhana's unjust war.

He fought valiantly on the Pandava side and was one of the few warriors who survived the war. After the war, he was appointed the guardian of Hastinapur by Yudhishthira during Parikshit's rule.

৪০

7. (D) Barbarik: Barbarik was the grandson of Bhima and son of Ghatotkacha, blessed with immense power. He was a great devotee of Lord Shiva and Goddess Kamakhya, and had received three powerful arrows — known as Teen Baan — that made him nearly invincible.

When the Kurukshetra war was about to begin, Barbarik vowed to fight for the weaker side. He rode to the battlefield on his blue horse, intending to observe which side was weaker before joining them.

Lord Krishna, curious and concerned about Barbarik's immense power, approached him in disguise. After testing his arrows, Krishna realized that Barbarik's vow could lead to a paradox: as he would keep switching sides (to always support the weaker one), he would end up destroying everyone, leaving only himself.

To prevent this, Krishna revealed his identity and asked for Barbarik's head as a donation (daan) — a supreme test of devotion and dharma. Barbarik willingly offered his head, fulfilling the ultimate act of sacrifice.

After his death, Krishna blessed him, saying that his head would watch the entire war from a hilltop and would be the first to witness Krishna's Vishvarupa. In Kali Yuga, Barbarik came to be worshipped as Khatu Shyam Ji in Rajasthan.

౧

8. (D) Babhruvahana: After the Kurukshetra war, when Yudhishthira was crowned king, the Ashwamedha Yagna (horse sacrifice ritual) was organized. Arjuna was sent to guard the ceremonial horse, which wandered into Manipura, ruled by Babruvahana — the son of Arjuna and Chitrangada (princess of Manipura).

Unaware of his lineage, Babruvahana challenged Arjuna as per the rules of the ritual. A fierce battle ensued, in which Babruvahana fatally wounded and killed Arjuna.

Stricken with grief, Chitrangada and Ulupi (Arjuna's other wife and a Naga princess) rushed to the scene. Ulupi used the Nagamani, a magical gem, to bring Arjuna back to life.

౧

9. (D) Sambha: Lakshmana, the daughter of Duryodhana, was known for her beauty and pride. Many royal suitors desired her hand in marriage, but her father, Duryodhana, planned a grand swayamvara (a ceremony where the bride chooses her husband).

However, Samba, the son of Lord Krishna and Jambavati, had already fallen in love with Lakshmana. Knowing that Duryodhana would never willingly agree to the match because of the rivalry between the Kauravas and

Krishna's family, Samba abducted Lakshmana from the ceremony.

Furious, Duryodhana and the Kauravas saw this as an insult. They captured Samba, brought him to Hastinapura, and imprisoned him.

When Lord Balarama, Krishna's elder brother, heard of this injustice, he went to Hastinapura to secure Samba's release. He was met with arrogance and refusal. In his anger, Balarama threatened to destroy the city with his plough (as he's also known as Halayudha – bearer of the plough).

Afraid of divine wrath, the Kauravas apologized and released Samba. Eventually, Duryodhana had to accept the marriage. Lakshmana and Samba were married with proper royal rites, bringing the episode to a dramatic but peaceful end.

QUIZ - 7: When God Walked the Earth

1. (A) Hayagriva: Two powerful asuras (demons) named Madhu and Kaitabha emerged from the earwax of Lord Vishnu while He was in deep cosmic slumber (yoga-nidra). They were born from the tamasic (dark) and rajasic (active) energies and possessed immense power. The two demons stole the Vedas, which contain the knowledge necessary for creation, and hid them deep in the cosmic ocean, creating chaos in the universe.

To restore balance and recover the sacred scriptures, Lord Vishnu took the form of Hayagriva, an incarnation with the body of a man and the head of a horse—symbolizing knowledge and intelligence. He descended into the depths of the ocean to retrieve the stolen Vedas.

Hayagriva engaged in a fierce battle with Madhu and Kaitabha that lasted for thousands of years. Due to their arrogance, the demons offered Vishnu a boon—mocking him, saying He could choose the time and place of their death. Seizing the opportunity, Lord Hayagriva chose to slay them at that very moment, when they were vulnerable. He then recovered the Vedas and restored them to Lord Brahma, enabling the continuation of creation.

2. (D) Rama: During their exile in the Dandaka forest, Rama, Sita, and Lakshmana were suddenly attacked by a terrifying demon named Viradha. This rakshasa was huge, invincible to weapons, and had received a boon that no weapon could kill him.

Viradha tried to abduct Sita, which enraged Rama and Lakshmana. Despite their arrows having no effect due to his boon, the brothers engaged in close combat. Realizing weapons wouldn't work, they uprooted a large tree and together buried Viradha alive in a deep pit, which ultimately ended the demon's life.

Before dying, Viradha revealed that he was actually a celestial being named Tumburu, cursed to be a demon. Rama's action freed him from the curse, and he ascended to the heavens, thanking the Lord.

ॐ

3. (C) Matsya: The first avatar of Lord Vishnu is Matsya, the fish incarnation.

At the end of a cosmic age, a great deluge threatened to destroy all life. Lord Vishnu took the form of a giant fish to save the sacred scriptures (Vedas), Sage Manu, and the seeds of all life. Matsya guided Manu's boat safely through the flood, preserving the world's knowledge and creation.

This avatar symbolizes protection, rebirth, and the preservation of dharma during times of chaos.

ॐ

4. (C) Narasimha: After Lord Vishnu took the fierce Narasimha form (half-man, half-lion) to slay the demon Hiranyakashipu, his rage became uncontrollable. Even after the demon's death, Narasimha continued roaring in fury, threatening to destroy the world.

The gods, unable to calm him, prayed to Lord Shiva. To pacify Narasimha and restore balance, Shiva took a terrifying form known as Sharabha — a mighty, part-lion, part-bird creature, stronger than Narasimha.

Sharabha subdued Narasimha and eventually calmed him down. In some versions, Narasimha merged back into Vishnu, while in others, Sharabha overpowered or even destroyed the furious form of Narasimha to save the cosmos.

%

5. (D) All of These: During the Mahabharata, three avatars of Lord Vishnu were present: Vyasa, who composed the epic and preserved sacred knowledge; Krishna, who guided the Pandavas and imparted the Bhagavad Gita's wisdom; and Parashurama, the warrior-sage who trained key fighters. Together, they played vital roles in upholding dharma during this epic age.

%

6. (B) Parshurama: Parashurama, the fierce warrior-sage and sixth avatar of Lord Vishnu, was a devoted disciple of Lord Shiva. Born as the son of sage Jamadagni, Parashurama sought Shiva's guidance to master powerful weapons and spiritual knowledge. Under Shiva's tutelage, he learned advanced martial arts, the use of divine weapons (including the axe), and profound yogic practices. Shiva's teachings transformed Parashurama into a formidable warrior destined to rid the world of corrupt and oppressive rulers, restoring dharma with both strength and wisdom.

%

7. (A) Nara-Narayana: Nar-Narayana are twin sages and divine incarnations of Lord Vishnu. They are considered manifestations of the supreme consciousness—Nara meaning "man" and Narayana meaning "the divine." According to legend, these two sages performed intense penance and meditation in the Himalayas to uphold dharma and cosmic order.

One of their famous abodes of penance is the sacred site of Kedarnath, where they meditated to seek Lord Shiva's blessings and spiritual strength. Their tapasya was so powerful that it resonated through the mountains, symbolizing the union of divine human effort and cosmic divinity.

Nar-Narayana's penance at Kedarnath highlights the ideal of devotion, asceticism, and the harmony between Vishnu and Shiva traditions. This story signifies the spiritual synergy where Vishnu devotees seek Shiva's grace to achieve ultimate liberation.

ಏ

8. (C) Vamana: King Bali was a mighty and generous demon king who ruled the three worlds with great power. His devotion and charity were unmatched, but his growing strength worried the gods. To restore cosmic balance, Lord Vishnu incarnated as Vamana, a dwarf Brahmin.

Vamana approached King Bali during a yajna (sacrifice) and asked for just three paces of land. Bali, known for his generosity, agreed. But then Vamana suddenly grew in size, becoming enormous—his first step covered the earth, the second the heavens. With no space left for the third, Bali offered his own head.

Vamana placed his third step on Bali's head, pushing him down to the netherworld, but spared him because of his humility and devotion. Bali was granted the boon to visit his people once a year, celebrated as the festival of Onam.

This story symbolizes the triumph of divine order and humility over pride and power.

ಜಿ

9. (C) Aditi: Devaki is regarded as an avatar of Goddess Aditi, the mother of the gods (Adityas) in Hindu mythology. Aditi is considered the cosmic mother and the personification of infinity and the eternal sky.

Devaki, the mother of Lord Krishna, is sometimes seen as the earthly incarnation of Aditi because just as Aditi gave birth to the celestial gods who maintain cosmic order, Devaki gave birth to Krishna, the divine protector and restorer of dharma (cosmic balance) on Earth. Thus, Devaki's role as Krishna's mother reflects Aditi's cosmic role as the source of divine power and sustenance.

This connection highlights the divine continuity from the cosmic to the earthly realm, emphasizing Devaki's sacred importance in the divine plan.

QUIZ - 8: Nine Goddesses, One Power

1. (D) Kushmanda: The fourth form of Goddess Durga is Kushmanda.

She is worshipped on the fourth day of Navaratri and is believed to be the creator of the universe. The name Kushmanda means "the cosmic egg" or "the creator of the cosmic light." According to mythology, she created the universe with her divine smile, filling it with energy and light.

Kushmanda is usually depicted with eight or ten hands, holding weapons and a rosary, seated on a lion, symbolizing strength and courage. She blesses her devotees with health, wealth, and prosperity.

2. (A) Dawon: The lion mount of Maa Parvati (Durga) is commonly known as Dawon or Somnandi. It is also referred to as Kesari in some traditions.

3. (C) Kaalratri: Goddess Kalaratri, a form of Durga, is also known as Shubhankari. Shubhankari means "the one who brings auspiciousness". She is revered as a fierce and protective deity, particularly on the seventh day of Navratri. Kalaratri is believed to be the destroyer of evil and darkness.

4. (B) Skandamata: Skandamata represents Veera Rasa (Heroism). She sends her young child, to whom she has passed on her courage, to fight a demon.

5. (D) Both (A) and (C): Shailaputri, the daughter of the mountains (Himalayas), is the first form of Goddess Durga worshipped on the first day of Navaratri. She appears dressed in pure white, symbolizing peace, purity, and innocence. Riding a gentle bull and holding a trident and a lotus, she represents the nurturing and steadfast energy of nature itself. White, in her form, reflects the calm and tranquil strength that lies within the foundation of all creation. She teaches devotees to start their spiritual journey with a pure heart and unwavering faith.

On the second day, Brahmacharini graces the devotees. Also clad in white, she embodies penance, devotion, and asceticism. Her serene appearance, holding a rosary and a water utensil, reflects a life dedicated to self-discipline and spiritual pursuit. The white attire again signifies purity—this time not just of the body, but of the mind and soul, emphasizing the importance of unwavering determination and sacrifice on the path to enlightenment.

Together, these two goddesses in white inspire us to embrace purity in thoughts and actions, while showing the strength found in calmness, devotion, and discipline. Their white clothes are a visual reminder of the sacred beginning of spiritual awakening, where peace and penance walk hand in hand.

6. (A) Chandraghanta: The third eye of the Chandraghanta form of Goddess Durga is always open. She is the third manifestation of Durga worshipped on the third day of Navratri, and is known for her fierce nature and readiness for battle. Chandraghanta's name means "one who has a half-moon shaped like a bell," and her third eye is constantly open, reflecting her unwavering vigilance and readiness to fight against demons.

❧

7. (B) Katyayni: The form of Goddess Durga who killed Mahishasura is Katyayni, also known as Mahishasuramardini, which means "Slayer of the buffalo demon Mahishasura."

Mahishasura was a powerful demon who could change his form at will and had been granted a boon that no man or god could kill him. Empowered by this boon, he began to terrorize the heavens and the Earth, defeating the gods and upsetting cosmic balance.

In response, the trinity of gods — Brahma, Vishnu, and Shiva — combined their divine energies to create a supreme goddess with unmatched power. This goddess was Durga, a fierce warrior with ten arms, each holding weapons gifted by different gods.

Mahishasura challenged Durga and fought fiercely, but she was unstoppable. After a long battle, she finally slew him, restoring peace and dharma to the world.

This victory is celebrated during the festival of Durga Puja and Navaratri, symbolizing the triumph of good over evil. Mahishasuramardini is often depicted riding a lion or tiger, with Mahishasura at her feet, representing her victory.

❧

8. (C) Himavan: Shailputri, the first form of Goddess Durga worshipped on the first day of Navratri, is the daughter of King Himavan, the personification of the Himalayas. Her name Shailputri literally means "Daughter of the Mountain."

In her previous birth, Goddess Shailputri was Sati, the daughter of Daksha Prajapati. Sati married Lord Shiva against her father's will. When Daksha organized a grand yagna but insulted Shiva by not inviting him, Sati could not bear the disrespect and immolated herself in the sacrificial fire. Heartbroken, Shiva withdrew into deep meditation carrying her burnt body.

In her next birth, Sati reincarnated as Parvati, the daughter of King Himavan and Queen Menavati. As Shailputri, she was born with divine grace and beauty, destined once again to become Shiva's consort. She performed deep penance to win Shiva's heart and was eventually reunited with him in marriage.

Thus, Shailputri represents strength, purity, and devotion, and is honored as the embodiment of nature itself, being born of the mighty Himalayas.

ॐ

9. (C) Siddhidatri: Siddhidatri represents Adbhuta Rasa (Wonder). She is the giver of powers, but even she is surprised by Brahma's creation of Prithvi Lok.

QUIZ - 9: *Where Shiva Dwells: The Luminous Shrines*

1. (B) Somnath: According to ancient scriptures, Soma, also known as Chandra Deva (the Moon God), was married to the 27 daughters of Daksha Prajapati. However, Soma showed special favor to one wife — Rohini, ignoring the others. Angered by his neglect, Daksha cursed Soma to lose his luster and fade away.

As Soma began to wane, the world fell into darkness and chaos. The devas advised him to worship Lord Shiva at Prabhas Teerth to be relieved from the curse. Chandra performed intense penance, and Lord Shiva appeared, restoring part of his brilliance and placing a limit on the curse — thus leading to the waxing and waning cycle of the moon.

To mark his divine appearance, Shiva manifested as a Jyotirlinga of radiant light, making Somnath the first of the twelve Jyotirlingas. The name "Somnath" means "Protector of Soma (Moon)".

ॐ

2. (A) Bhimashankar: The Bhimashankar Jyotirlinga Temple's story is linked to the myth of Bhimasur, the son of the demon Kumbhakarna. Bhimasur, enraged by his father's death at the hands of Lord Rama, performed severe penance to gain immense power from Lord Brahma. He then terrorized the land, but Lord Shiva, as Bhimashankar, defeated him and restored peace. The temple's location in the Sahyadri hills is also linked to a battle between Lord Shiva and the demon Tripurasura, according to Shiv Shankar Tirth Yatra.

ॐ

3. (C) Ghrishneshwar: The Grishneshwar Jyotirlinga is situated in the village of Verul, approximately 30 kilometers northwest of Aurangabad in the Chhatrapati Sambhajinagar district of Maharashtra, India. It is located near the UNESCO World Heritage site of the Ellora Caves, making it a significant pilgrimage destination for devotees of Lord Shiva.

Grishneshwar is considered the 12th and final Jyotirlinga among the twelve sacred shrines dedicated to Lord Shiva. The temple is associated with a poignant legend from the Shiva Purana:

A devoted woman named Ghushma used to create 101 Shivalingas from clay, worship them, and immerse them in a nearby lake. Her sister, driven by jealousy, killed Ghushma's son and threw his body into the same lake. Despite her grief, Ghushma continued her daily rituals. Moved by her unwavering devotion, Lord Shiva restored her son to life and manifested himself as a Jyotirlinga at that spot, known as Grishneshwar, meaning "Lord of Compassion"

ॐ

4. (C) Khandwa: The Omkareshwar Jyotirlinga is located on the Mandhata (or Shivapuri) Island in the Narmada River, in Khandwa district, Madhya Pradesh, India.

ॐ

5. (D) Kedarnath: After the devastating Kurukshetra war, the Pandavas were burdened with guilt for killing their kin and Brahmins. To atone for their sins, they sought the blessings of Lord Shiva, the lord of destruction and transformation. However, Shiva, angered by the bloodshed, avoided them and took the form of a bull, hiding in the Garhwal region.

The Pandavas chased him to the Himalayas. Bhima, one of the Pandava brothers, spotted the bull grazing. When he tried to catch it, the bull dove into the ground. Bhima held onto its tail and hind legs, but the rest of the body disappeared into the earth. Impressed by their devotion and repentance, Shiva finally forgave them and appeared in his true form.

It is said that the hump of the bull appeared in Kedarnath, and the Pandavas built a temple over it — which is the Kedarnath Jyotirlinga. Other parts of Shiva's body are believed to have appeared at Tungnath (arms), Rudranath (face), Madhyamaheshwar (navel), and Kalpeshwar (hair) — together known as the Panch Kedar temples.

ॐ

6. (A) Godavari: The Godavari River flows near the Trimbakeshwar Jyotirlinga in Trimbak, Maharashtra. The Godavari is considered one of the holiest rivers in India, often referred to as the "Dakshin Ganga" (Ganges of the South). It originates from the Brahmagiri Hills, just behind the Trimbakeshwar Temple. According to legend, it was Lord Shiva who brought the river to Earth at the request of the sage Gautama. The presence of the Godavari's source makes Trimbakeshwar not only a Jyotirlinga site but also a significant pilgrimage spot for river worship.

ॐ

7. (B) Baidyanath: Ravana, a great devotee of Lord Shiva, performed intense penance to please him. Pleased by his devotion, Shiva offered him a boon. Ravana requested to take Shiva with him to Lanka. Shiva agreed but gave him a Shivalinga (believed to be a Jyotirlinga) with a condition: if the linga was placed on the ground, it would remain there forever. On his journey, Ravana needed to relieve himself and asked a shepherd boy (who was actually Lord Vishnu in disguise) to hold the linga. The boy tricked Ravana by placing the linga on the ground, and it got firmly established there. Furious but helpless, Ravana tried to uproot it, damaging it in the process. That Shivalinga came to be worshipped as Baidyanath (Baijnath) Jyotirlinga, signifying Shiva as the "Lord of Healing"

8. (A) Nageshwar: The Nageshwar Jyotirlinga Temple's story revolves around a demon named Daruka and a Shiva devotee named Supriya. Daruka, though a devotee of Shiva, was a cruel demon who imprisoned Supriya. Supriya's unwavering devotion to Shiva, even while being tortured, impressed the god, who manifested as Nageshwar to vanquish Daruka and reside there.

Nageshwar Jyotirlinga is situated about 17–18 km from Dwarka on the route to Bet Dwarka, making it a prominent pilgrimage site for devotees visiting the westernmost part of India.

9. (C) Mahakaleshwar: The Mahakaleshwar Jyotirlinga is situated on the banks of the holy river Shipra in Ujjain, Madhya Pradesh.

QUIZ - 10: *The Divine Assembly*

1. (B) Nahusha: Nahusha was a mighty king and a descendant of the Kuru dynasty, making him an ancestor of the Pandavas. When Indra, the king of heaven, went into hiding after slaying the demon Vritra, the gods appointed Nahusha as the temporary ruler of heaven. Elevated to this high position, Nahusha grew arrogant and prideful. His hubris led him to disrespect sages and even attempt to dominate the great sage Agastya. As a result, Agastya cursed Nahusha to fall from heaven and become a serpent, condemning him to live on earth in a lowly form. Nahusha's story serves as a lesson on the dangers of pride and the importance of humility, even for the most powerful beings.

2. (D) Both (A) and (B): Daksha and Ganesha's Curses on Chandra – The Moon God

1. Daksha's Curse: Once, Chandra, the Moon God, married Daksha Prajapati's 27 daughters, who are the 27 Nakshatras (lunar constellations). However, Chandra favored only one of them—Rohini—and neglected the others. This partiality deeply hurt the other wives, who complained to their father, Daksha. Angered by Chandra's behavior, Daksha cursed him to lose his brilliance and beauty, causing the Moon to wane and eventually disappear. Chandra, now weak and fading, sought Lord Shiva's help. Shiva partially lifted the curse by granting him the power to regain his light in phases, leading to the waxing and waning cycle of the Moon. This is why the Moon grows and diminishes in

brightness over the month.

2. Ganesha's Curse:On Ganesh Chaturthi, Lord Ganesha was once returning home after feasting on sweets. He was riding his mouse when he stumbled and fell. Chandra Deva, watching from the sky, laughed at Ganesha's form and fall. Offended, Ganesha cursed Chandra, saying, "You shall lose your beauty and brilliance, and anyone who looks at you on Ganesh Chaturthi will be falsely accused of wrongdoing." Chandra apologized and repented. Ganesha, compassionate, softened the curse, but decreed that looking at the Moon on Ganesh Chaturthi may still cause false accusations.

3. (D) All of These: Surya, the Sun God, is father to several notable figures in Hindu mythology, including Shani, Karna, and Sugriva. Shani, born to Surya and Chhaya, is the stern god of justice who governs karma and human destiny. Karna, son of Surya and Kunti, is a heroic yet tragic warrior famed for his bravery and generosity in the Mahabharata. Sugriva, a monkey king and ally of Lord Rama in the Ramayana, also traces his lineage to Surya, symbolizing leadership and loyalty. Together, these sons reflect Surya's diverse divine qualities across different epics.

4. (A) Varuna: Makara, a sea creature often depicted as a half-crocodile and half-fish or half-elephant beast, is the vahana (vehicle) of Varuna, the Vedic god of water, oceans, and cosmic order.

5. (C) Kama: Kamadeva, the god of love, was previously burned to ashes by Lord Shiva's third eye when he tried to disrupt Shiva's meditation. However, Rati, Kamadeva's wife, was devastated and prayed for her husband's rebirth.

It was prophesied that Kamadeva would be reborn as the son of Lord Vishnu. Fulfilling this prophecy, Kamadeva was reborn as Pradyumna, the son of Krishna (an avatar of Vishnu) and Rukmini, Krishna's chief consort.

Soon after his birth, the demon Shambara, fearing a prophecy that Pradyumna would kill him, kidnapped the infant and threw him into the ocean. A fish swallowed the child, and this fish was later caught and brought to Shambara's kitchen. There, Mayavati—a form of Rati—was working, and she recognized the child as her husband reborn.

She raised him in secret, and as he grew, Pradyumna regained his divine powers. Eventually, he killed Shambara, fulfilling the prophecy, and returned to Dwarka, reuniting with Krishna and Rukmini.

෨ඁ

6. (B) Bheema: Kunti, the mother of the Pandavas, had received a boon from Sage Durvasa in her youth. This boon allowed her to invoke any deity and bear a child from them.

After her marriage to King Pandu, who had been cursed that he would die if he ever engaged in intimacy, Kunti used this boon to bear children without violating the curse. To fulfill Pandu's wish for strong and heroic sons, Kunti invoked Vayu Deva, the wind god.

Vayu appeared and blessed Kunti with a powerful child. Thus, Bhima was born, infused with the strength and might of the wind. From birth, he displayed immense physical strength, and as he grew, he became the strongest among the Pandavas.

๛

7. (A) Vritrasura: Vritra was a powerful asura (demon) and a personification of drought and obstruction. He had gained a boon that he could not be killed by any weapon made of metal or wood, or during day or night, or by any conventional means. He also had a promise from the gods that he wouldn't be attacked unfairly.

Indra, the king of the Devas, approached Sage Dadhichi, who willingly sacrificed his body so that his bones could be used to create the Vajra, a divine weapon.

However, in some later retellings, when Indra couldn't defeat Vritra head-on due to his immense power and protections, he struck him from behind, violating the code of fair warfare, and ultimately killed him.

This act brought disapproval even among the gods, and Indra had to go into hiding to atone for this adharmic act, eventually being purified and restored.

๛

8. (C) Vinata: Vinata was one of the wives of Sage Kashyapa and the mother of two important celestial beings — Aruna and Garuda.

Vinata and her Kadru both wished for powerful children. Kadru wished for a thousand Nāga (serpent) sons, while Vinata asked for just two mighty sons. Kashyapa granted both their wishes.

Kadru's eggs hatched first, and her sons were born. Vinata, impatient and eager, broke one of her eggs before the proper time. From it emerged Aruna, not fully developed. Angry at being born prematurely, Aruna cursed his mother that she would become a slave to Kadru for her impatience, but also assured her that her second son, Garuda, would one day free her.

Later, Aruna grew into a powerful radiant being and was appointed as the charioteer of the Sun God (Suryadev), as he could withstand the intense brilliance of the sun and guide the divine chariot across the sky.

Thus, Vinata became the revered mother of Aruna, the eternal dawn and divine charioteer of the Sun.

ॐ

9. (D) Skanda: Long ago, the demon Tarakasura was granted a boon that only the son of Lord Shiva could kill him. Confident that Shiva would never marry again after the loss of Sati, Tarakasura grew arrogant and began terrorizing the heavens, defeating even the gods.

To protect the universe, the gods urged Shiva to marry Parvati, the reincarnation of Sati. After deep penance and devotion, Parvati won Shiva's heart, and their divine union led to the birth of Kartikeya — a radiant and powerful warrior.

As Kartikeya grew, his valor and intelligence became evident. He was soon chosen by the gods as their Senapati (commander-in-chief) to lead the army against Tarakasura. Riding his peacock and armed with the divine Vel (spear), Kartikeya led the celestial forces into battle.

In a fierce confrontation, Kartikeya ultimately slew Tarakasura, fulfilling the prophecy. His bravery and leadership earned him the eternal position as the Supreme Commander of the Devas.

QUIZ - 11: *Lords of Ego and Ambition*

1. (D) Tarakasura: Tarakasura was a powerful demon who received a boon from Lord Brahma that he could only be killed by the son of Lord Shiva. Confident in his immortality, Tarakasura wreaked havoc across the heavens and earth, believing no one could defeat him as Shiva was an ascetic and had no children.

To end Tarakasura's tyranny, the gods prayed to Lord Shiva to marry and have a son who could destroy the demon. Lord Shiva married Goddess Parvati, and their son Kartikeya (also called Skanda or Murugan) was born.

Kartikeya grew up to be a fierce warrior and led the divine army to battle Tarakasura, ultimately defeating and killing him, thus restoring peace and balance.

2. (D) Both (B) and (C): Putana, the demoness who tried to kill baby Krishna, had several powerful demon brothers in Hindu mythology. Her most well-known brothers are:

1. Bakasura - A monstrous crane demon who tried to devour Krishna and was killed by him.

2. Aghasura - A serpent demon (nāga) who assumed the form of a gigantic snake to swallow Krishna and his friends, but was also slain by Krishna.

These three — Putana, Bakasura, and Aghasura — were siblings and key allies of Kamsa, the evil king of Mathura, who sent them to kill Krishna, fearing the prophecy of his death at Krishna's hands.

3. (B) Ravana: Jaya and Vijaya, in their first life during Satya Yuga, were born as Hiranyaksha (Vijaya) and Hiranyakashipu (Jaya) to Diti (daughter of Daksha Prajapati) and sage Kashyapa. Hiranyaksha was killed by Varaha (boar avatar) and Hiranyakashipu was killed by Narasimha (man-lion avatar). In their second life during the Treta Yuga, they were born as Ravana (Jaya) and Kumbhakarna (Vijaya), and both were killed by Rama. In their third life during Dvapara Yuga, they were born as Shishupala (Jaya) and Dantavakra (Vijaya) and both were killed by Krishna. In their first two births, they were brothers, and in their final birth, they were cousins.

4. (C) Kumbhakarna: Jaya and Vijaya, in their first life during Satya Yuga, were born as Hiranyaksha (Vijaya) and Hiranyakashipu (Jaya) to Diti (daughter of Daksha Prajapati) and sage Kashyapa. Hiranyaksha was killed by Varaha (boar avatar) and Hiranyakashipu was killed by Narasimha (man-lion avatar). In their second life during the Treta Yuga, they were born as Ravana (Jaya) and Kumbhakarna (Vijaya), and both were killed by Rama. In their third life during Dvapara Yuga, they were born as Shishupala (Jaya) and Dantavakra (Vijaya) and both were killed by Krishna. In their first two births, they were brothers, and in their final birth, they were cousins.

5. (A) Vrinda: Vrinda was a devoted wife and a powerful devotee of Lord Vishnu. She was married to the demon king Jalandhar, and her unwavering chastity and devotion protected him from defeat in battle. To help the gods defeat Jalandhar, Lord Vishnu took the form of Jalandhar and deceived Vrinda, breaking her purity. When Vrinda realized the deception, she cursed Vishnu to lose his earthly form and suffer separation from his wife. Filled with sorrow and anger, Vrinda then immolated herself.

Because of this curse, Vishnu's earthly incarnation as Rama had to endure separation from his wife Sita. This story highlights the power of devotion and chastity as well as the complexities of divine play (leela) in Hindu mythology.

6. (B) Hanuman: Makardhwaja was the son of Lord Hanuman. His birth story is quite unique. After Lord Hanuman burned the demon king Ravana's city of Lanka with his fiery tail, he jumped into the ocean to cool himself. During this, a drop of Hanuman's sweat fell into the mouth of a mighty fish called a Makara (a sea creature).

This Makara later gave birth to a son, who was named Makardhwaja, meaning "born from the Makara." Though Hanuman was unaware of his son, Makardhwaja grew up to become a great warrior and served in the kingdom of his father's devotees.

Thus, Makardhwaja is considered Hanuman's son, born in an extraordinary way.

7. (D) All of These: All - Mahishasura, Shumbha and Munda, got the boon from Lord Brahma that they couldn't die at the hands of any male (human or god), or animal. Therefore, all were eventually destined to die at the hands of the Goddess.

8. (A) Hunda: Ashok Sundari, the daughter of Lord Shiva and Goddess Parvati, was born from the Kalpavriksha (wish-fulfilling tree) to bring joy and companionship to Parvati. She was destined to marry Nahusha, a mighty king of the lunar dynasty.

One day, Ashok Sundari was roaming near Mount Mandara when she encountered a demon named Hunda, who was captivated by her beauty. He proposed marriage, but Ashok Sundari firmly rejected him, stating she was destined to marry Nahusha.

Enraged and humiliated by her refusal, Hunda tried to abduct her. But Ashok Sundari, being divine and powerful, cursed Hunda — declaring that he would be killed by her future husband, Nahusha.

Fearing the curse, Hunda later tried to kill Nahusha in his childhood, but failed. As fate had it, Nahusha eventually grew up and fulfilled the curse by slaying Hunda, thus ending the demon's reign of terror and fulfilling the divine prophecy.

ॐ

9. (C) Banasura: Usha, the daughter of the powerful demon king Banasura, once had a dream of a handsome young prince. Captivated by the vision, she longed to find and meet him. With the help of her friend Chitralekha, a skilled artist and magician, Usha's dream prince was identified as Aniruddha—the grandson of Lord Krishna.

Using her magical powers, Chitralekha brought Aniruddha to Usha's palace secretly. The two instantly fell in love and got married in private. When Banasura discovered this secret union, he was furious. Being a mighty warrior blessed by Lord Shiva, Banasura opposed the marriage and captured Aniruddha.

To rescue his grandson, Lord Krishna led an army to fight Banasura. A fierce battle ensued between Krishna and Banasura, who was protected by Shiva's blessings. Ultimately, Krishna's forces triumphed, and Aniruddha was freed.

The story symbolizes love transcending boundaries, uniting even demon and divine bloodlines, and the victory of devotion and righteousness over enmity.

QUIZ - 12: *Sacred MInds, Silent Power: The Ancient Sages*

1. (A) Shakuntala: Shakuntala was born to Vishwamitra and Menaka, a celestial apsara. Menaka had been sent by the gods to distract Vishwamitra from his intense penance. As a result of their union, Shakuntala was born. However, Menaka left the newborn near the hermitage of Sage Kanva, who raised her as his own daughter.

Shakuntala later married King Dushyanta, and their son Bharata became a legendary emperor, after whom India is named (Bharatavarsha). Her story is famously told in the Mahabharata

ॐ

2. (C) Bhrigu: Sage Bhrigu, one of the ancient Saptarishis, is honored as the father of Hindu astrology. Gifted with deep insight into the cosmos, he compiled the Bhrigu Samhita, a vast astrological manuscript that recorded the destinies of countless individuals based on the positions of planets at their birth. Through intense meditation and study, Bhrigu understood how celestial bodies influence human lives and futures. His pioneering work laid the foundation for Vedic astrology, guiding generations to read the stars and seek knowledge of their destiny.

ॐ

3. (C) Kanava: Shakuntala was adopted by the sage Kanva. After her birth, Shakuntala's mother, the celestial nymph Menaka, left her in the forest. Sage Kanva found the infant and raised her in his hermitage, nurturing her with love and wisdom. Shakuntala grew up there, away from worldly distractions, until she later met King Dushyanta, leading to the famous tale of love and separation in the Mahabharata and Kalidasa's classic play Abhijnanashakuntalam.

4. (D) All of These:

1. Daksha - Daksha's anger stemmed from his belief that Shiva was unsuitable as a husband for Sati. He criticized Shiva's appearance and lifestyle, deeming him disrespectful and inauspicious. Daksha declared that no offerings would be made to Shiva and that Shiva's followers would be expelled from Vedic rites, condemning them to heretical behavior.

2. Kashyapa - Rishi Kashyap cursed Lord Shiva after witnessing Shiva behead Surya Dev. Surya Dev was beheaded when Shiva struck him with his trident to defend devotees. Witnessing his son's condition, Sage Kashyap cursed Shiva, prophesying that Shiva would one day harm his own son. This prophecy was fulfilled when Shiva was forced to behead Ganesha.

5. (B) Parashara: Vyasa, the great sage and author of the Mahabharata, was born to the sage Parashara. Parashara was a highly revered rishi known for his wisdom and spiritual powers.

According to legend, Parashara was traveling through a forest when he came across a young maiden named Satyavati, daughter of a fisherman. Satyavati was known for her enchanting fragrance and beauty. Parashara was captivated by her and wished to be with her. Satyavati was hesitant but agreed after Parashara promised that her virginity would remain intact and that she would gain eternal youth and fragrance.

From this union, Vyasa was born. Vyasa grew up to become a legendary sage, composer of the Vedas, and the epic Mahabharata.

❀

6. (A) Pulastya: Ravana, the mighty king of Lanka, hailed from a powerful lineage of sages and gods. His grandfather was Sage Pulastya, one of the ten Prajapatis (mind-born sons of Brahma) and a revered sage in Hindu mythology.

Pulastya was known for his great wisdom and austerity. He played a key role in the divine genealogy as the father of Sage Vishrava, who was Ravana's father. Vishrava married Kaikesi, a rakshasi princess, and together they had Ravana, Kumbhakarna, and Vibhishana.

Thus, Ravana's grandfather Pulastya's spiritual legacy and strength were passed down through the generations, shaping Ravana's immense power and knowledge.

❀

7. (C) Parshurama: Karna, eager to learn warfare and celestial weapons, approached Parashurama, the great warrior-sage and avatar of Vishnu. Knowing that Parashurama taught only Brahmins, Karna lied about his identity, claiming to be a Brahmin.

Parashurama accepted him as a disciple and trained him rigorously. Karna proved to be a brilliant student and earned his teacher's praise.

One afternoon, Parashurama was resting with his head on Karna's lap. At that moment, an insect burrowed into Karna's thigh, causing immense pain. Yet, Karna remained still, so as not to disturb his guru's sleep. When Parashurama awoke and saw the blood, he realized Karna couldn't be a Brahmin, for only a Kshatriya could endure such agony without flinching.

Furious at the deception, Parashurama cursed Karna: When you most need the knowledge I have given you—at a critical moment in battle—you will forget it.

This curse later came true during Karna's final battle with Arjuna in the Kurukshetra War, leading to his tragic downfall.

ॐ

8. (D) Markandeya: The Mahamrityunjaya Mantra is written by Rishi Markandeya, a great sage in Hindu mythology.

According to legend, Sage Markandeya composed and chanted this powerful mantra to worship Lord Shiva and seek his protection from death (mrityu). The mantra appears in the Rigveda (Mandala 7, Hymn 59, Verse 12) and is also found in the Yajurveda.

It is believed that chanting this mantra can overcome fear, protect against untimely death, and bring physical, mental, and spiritual healing.

ॐ

9. (D) All of These: Vyasa, Kripacharya, and Markandeya are considered Chiranjivis (immortals) in Hindu tradition due to their exceptional spiritual merit and divine roles. Vyasa remains alive to preserve and spread sacred knowledge as the author of the Mahabharata and Vedas.

Kripacharya was blessed with immortality for his righteousness and continued role as a teacher and guide. Markandeya, a symbol of unwavering devotion, was saved from death by Lord Shiva and lives on as an eternal sage. Their immortality serves to uphold dharma, wisdom, and devotion across the ages.